The Good State

Other books by the same author

ACADEMIC
An Introduction to Philosophical Logic
The Refutation of Scepticism
Berkeley: The Central Arguments
Wittgenstein
Russell
Philosophy 1: A Guide through the Subject (editor)
Philosophy 2: Further through the Subject (editor)
The Continuum Encyclopedia of British Philosophy (editor)
Truth, Meaning and Realism
Scepticism and the Possibility of Knowledge
The History of Philosophy

GENERAL
The Long March to the Fourth of June (with Xu You Yu, as Li Xiao Jun)
China: A Literary Companion (with Susan Whitfield)
The Future of Moral Values
The Quarrel of the Age: The Life and Times of William Hazlitt
Herrick: Lyrics of Love and Desire (editor)
What Is Good?
Descartes: The Life and Times of a Genius
Among the Dead Cities
Against All Gods
Towards the Light
The Choice of Hercules
Ideas that Matter
To Set Prometheus Free
Liberty in the Age of Terror
The Good Book
The God Argument
A Handbook of Humanism (editor, with Andrew Copson)
Friendship
The Age of Genius
War
Democracy and Its Crisis

ESSAY COLLECTIONS
The Meaning of Things
The Reason of Things
The Mystery of Things
The Heart of Things
The Form of Things
Thinking of Answers
The Challenge of Things

The Good State

On the Principles of Democracy

A. C. GRAYLING

ONEWORLD

A Oneworld Book

First published by Oneworld Publications, 2020

ISBN 978-1-78607-718-9
eISBN 978-1-78607-719-6

Typeset by Hewer Text UK Ltd
Printed and bound in Great Britain by Clays Ltd, Elcograf S.p.A.

Oneworld Publications
10 Bloomsbury Street, London, WC1B 3SR, England
3754 Pleasant Ave, Suite 100, Minneapolis, MN 55409, USA

For Eva

— No sé qué opinará usted, pero a mí me parece que un país civilizado es aquel en que uno no tiene necesidad de perder el tiempo con la política.

Javier Cercas, *Soldados de Salamina*

CONTENTS

PREFACE

What principles must a political and constitutional order be based upon if it is to be democratic? The following pages answer this question. The answer is given by an examination of what the concept of democracy itself entails. The point of asking the question is that even those states standardly described as the 'world's leading democracies' do not meet the requirements that the principles of democracy impose.

This is a large claim, but if right it is too important to ignore. In a previous book, *Democracy and Its Crisis* (2017), I discussed the problems that democracy is facing, especially in what are taken to be two key exemplars of the model: the United States and the United Kingdom. That book outlines what a 'representative democracy' is meant to be, how and why the conception of such a democracy arose, and how and why it has lately gone astray.[1] In my judgment the case for representative democracy is better than for 'direct', 'sortitive', 'deliberative', and other versions of democracy, and therefore it is worth defending not just from external attack, but – equally importantly – from the corrosive influence of inherent and acquired internal inadequacies which need to be identified and remedied to preserve the good offered by democracy as such.[2]

The present book is a contribution to this latter task. I undertake it by seeking to make clear the fundamental principles on which a political and constitutional order must be based in order to be democratic in the full meaning of this term. The task is an urgent one, because many more democracies than just the two mentioned are at risk from the absence or decay of the fundamental principles at issue, an absence or decay that developments over the last few years have exposed. We have learned from these developments that there is a ticking time-bomb at the heart of a major form of representative democracy – the 'Westminster Model' and its derivatives and developments (of which the US Constitution is a variant) – in more than fifty countries around the world. The problem is as large and as widespread as it is serious.

This is not a book about constitutional technicalities, although the points I make are illuminated by reference to aspects both of Westminster Model constitutions and those of other democracies.[3] Instead this is a book about *principles*, the principles that should underlie a democratic order. It is an answer to the question, What should a democratic order be like in its fundamentals, to ensure that it delivers what democracy is meant to be for? Nevertheless, certain of the fundamental principles directly speak to the question of what a constitution *must* contain, constraining what any individual constitution for a democratic order can be like. These principles are violated by the very nature of the Westminster Model, so even in countries which have developed and improved that model in a number of respects – compare the Australian constitutional arrangements to the British, for such an example – they have not defused the time-bomb at the model's heart. So I repeat: the problem addressed here is as large and widespread as it is serious.

But this discussion of principles is not intended to be abstract and theoretical merely. Theorizing may have its pleasures, but its terminus is too often the ever-receding utopian horizon which, for the serious business of government and its impact on human realities, is not the right destination. Practical remedies are needed to make democracy deliver its promise of being *by the people, for the people.* These remedies have to be formulated in response to identified and diagnosed weaknesses in the democratic systems that have evolved over the last two centuries, this evolution having mainly been controlled by those in positions of influence so that they could reduce the extent to which their own power was attenuated. Frustration with the imposed filters that thus increasingly dilute 'people power' the further up the hierarchies of governmental and legislative institutions one goes, prompts some to clutch at radical and dramatic alternatives.[4] This is to risk throwing the baby out with the bathwater, because much in the hard-won democratic advances made over the last two centuries is worth preserving. The better metaphor here is that of a journey, and to say that it has not yet reached its goal, which is: a reliable, well-functioning order that meets the fundamental democratic demand that government, constituted by the authority of the people and answerable to them, exists to serve the people's interests – all the people. There is very much more to this simple and obvious-seeming formula than at first meets the eye, as the following pages are designed to show.

ACKNOWLEDGEMENTS

I have benefitted greatly from conversations with Lord Lisvane, former Clerk to the House of Commons, whose knowledge on constitutional and parliamentary matters is second to none, and Sir Geoffrey Palmer, former Prime Minister of New Zealand, who has been at work on proposals for constitutional reform in his home country for a number of years. Neither is responsible for any of the views expressed in these pages. In the course of having the interesting privilege of chairing the 'Where Next' group on Brexit 2017–2019, I had occasion to learn from the views of a number of parliamentarians, among them Dominic Grieve MP, Caroline Lucas MP, Chuka Umunna MP, Tom Brake MP, Phillip Lee MP, Lord Kerr of Kinlochard, Lord Dykes of Harrow, Lord Newby, Lord Adonis, Baroness Wheatcroft, Baroness Ludford, Richard Corbett MEP, Catherine Bearder MEP, Edward McMillan-Scott former MEP – these in person, and many others in correspondence. Also, from Peter Kellner and Timothy Garton-Ash both in conversation and in reading their work; from Vernon Bogdanor's writings and earlier conversations at the New College of the Humanities; and from numerous others of whom considerations of space prevent mention. To all of these I am grateful. None of them has any responsibility for the views in what follows, and indeed many of them would vigorously disagree with at least some of those views. I am, however, confident that all those named here would agree that the issues raised are important, and need addressing – all the more so because of the constitutional difficulties attending the Brexit process in the UK, the analogous implications of the Trump presidency in the United States, and the significance of both for representative democracy in general and Westminster Model versions in particular.

INTRODUCTION

This book examines a specific question: What principles must underlie any political and governmental order which receives its legitimacy, its powers, the extent and conditions of their exercise, and the fundamental purposes they serve, from the active consent of the governed, whose rights, interests and well-being are at stake in giving that consent? It is therefore an examination of what, in the broadest sense, is to be described as the fundamental principles of democracy.

Apart from the intrinsic importance of such an examination, there is an acute need for it, as revealed by an analysis of a dominant constitutional model on which many democracies are based. This is the 'Westminster Model', examples of which – or derivations from which – exist in the United Kingdom, Australia, Canada, New Zealand, India, Ireland, and nearly fifty other states including (for reasons that will be explained) the United States and other countries which have modified the Westminster Model into a presidential or hybrid form. Not least because of the influence once exerted in the world by governments based in Westminster when it ruled an extensive empire, this model is apt to proclaim itself, in self-congratulatory terms, as the very type of a system designed to foster good governance. The proceedings in the Westminster Parliament – 'the mother of Parliaments' – would be recognizable today to an MP who sat in it in the age of Gladstone and Disraeli, and this fact might be cited with approval by one who is persuaded of the perfection of its forms and the value of continuity. Instead this fact should be taken as symptomatic of problems, which in several ways infect democracies around the world.

This is because Westminster Model democracy, both in its place of origin and in many of the political and governmental orders derived from it, is either dysfunctional or in danger of becoming so as a result of the model's essential weaknesses. The phenomenon of 'Brexit' in the United Kingdom exposed those weaknesses, sending an urgent alarm signal to all the democracies which imitate or descend from it. These weaknesses therefore illustrate, by way of what is needed to put them right, the requisites of a satisfactory democratic order. The immediate implication of these considerations is the need for significant reform in nearly all contemporary Westminster Model polities.[1]

Almost every term used in the first paragraph of this introduction – 'legitimacy', 'powers', 'consent', 'rights', and others – requires clarification and, in important cases, defence. Both are given in what follows. I shall focus principally on the United Kingdom and United States because they exemplify the most egregious failings of different forms of the model; but reference is made to its operation elsewhere in the world in further support of the argument.[2]

The problems with Westminster Model democracies fall into two classes: those that concern the *institutions* characteristic of the model, and those that concern the *practices and personnel* characteristic of the model. Both raise questions about the constitutional arrangements governing them.

On the *institutional* side of the question, the most important points relate to the separation of functions and powers among executive, legislature, and judiciary; the nature of the institutions whose purpose is the exercise of these functions and powers; the duties, extent, and limits of the functions and powers of each branch and the people who operate it, and the manner and form of the definition of these functions and powers; the system of representation; and the rights of citizens, together with the remedies for any violation of such rights.

Underlying all this are the crucial questions of the *purpose of government* and what this entails for each of these matters, and the *principles* that underlie the constitutional provisions for each of them.

On the side of the question relating to the *practices and personnel* of a democracy, the most important points relate to politicians and the nature of party politics, the traditions and non-constitutional practices of the legislative and executive arms, party-political activity outside the legislative and executive institutions, and the press and other media.

I shall call the institutional side of the question the *formal* side, and the 'people and practices' side the *informal* side for brevity hereafter. I deal with the formal side mainly in chapters 2, 3, 5, and 6, and the informal side mainly in chapters 4 and 8. They cannot be kept wholly apart, not least because formal arrangements are often needed to control the possible effects of what can happen on the informal side.

It will be seen that there are tensions between the two sides of the question, as well as flaws internal to each. This point is significant because it warns us that a *constitution* – even a clear, consistent, principled, and detailed one that defines the duties, extent, and limits of government and how it is to be carried out in the interests of the state and its people – is not by itself a guarantee

3

that those interests will be served. There are many countries in the world with excellent formal constitutions which are not observed in practice, because their high-sounding intentions are ignored or subverted as a result of what happens on the informal side of the question. The contrast between the constitutions of today's People's Republic of China and Russian Federation and the activities of their governments and security services offers contemporary edifying examples. Many more could be cited.

But a clear, consistent, and principled constitution is a necessity nevertheless. At the beginning of Book 2 of his *Ab Urbe Condita* (From the Founding of the City), the Roman historian Livy says that the ending of kingly rule, achieved by expelling the haughty Tarquins, enabled 'the authority of the law to be exalted above that of men' in the Roman republic thus instituted.[3] By 'law' in this context Livy meant a constitutional framework; laws as such are not invariably instruments of justice, and indeed can be oppressive and unjust (think 'apartheid laws' in South Africa, 'Nuremberg Laws' and other legal disabilities of Jews in Nazi Germany). But given that it is a constitution-forming legal order which, along with other conventions and traditions, governs the institutions and practices of a state, the crucial question becomes: What is a *good* constitution? What principles should govern its formulation and application, and how are they in turn to be justified?

The idea of the 'authority of law above that of men' in Livy's sense encapsulates the purpose of a constitution, which is to define and therefore limit the competencies of those entrusted with the exercise of legislative and executive powers. In an absolute monarchy there are no such constraints; that is what 'absolute' means, and it therefore further means 'arbitrary' and 'unrestrained' – though even defenders of absolutism such as Jacques-Bénigne Bossuet, apologist for the rule of Louis XIV of

France, sought to temper absolutism by appeal to the idea that a monarch remains answerable to something putatively higher: to moral principles, or a deity.[4] In practice throughout history, as the sufferings of too many in humanity testify, such appeals have been less than universally successful. An important part of the reason is captured in Lord Acton's dictum, 'Power tends to corrupt, and absolute power corrupts absolutely.' But we tend to overlook the significance of the first part of that dictum, 'Power tends to corrupt': it is not only absolute power that does so. Hence the importance of constitutional restraints; and hence the uncomfortable fact that even excellent constitutions can be nullified by what happens on the informal side of politics and government.

This is where a thought prompted by John Stuart Mill becomes relevant. In his book *Considerations on Representative Government* (1861) he invoked, more or less in passing, the idea of 'constitutional morality' as what restrains honourable men (in his day, and despite his protests, it was of course only men – apart from the Queen – who engaged in politics and government) from bending or manipulating, for partisan or injurious purposes, the conventions, traditions, and provisions of the constitutional order, then as now in the UK an uncodified one.[5] There is an echo in this of Voltaire's remark about the England of the preceding century, where he had lived for some years in exile, namely, that its liberties were the result 'not of the constitution (governmental arrangements) of the country but the constitution (character) of the people' – that is, the people's robust insistence on the inviolability of their persons and homes.[6] Mill took it, in nineteenth-century style, that it was the principles of gentlemanly behaviour that prevented governments from exercising through Parliament what were in fact – and which in the UK remain today – absolute powers.

But this is a very tenuous way of constraining what governments and their ministers can do, unhappily made obvious
when the legislature and government offices come to be populated by less honourable and principled people, controlled by
party machines whose influence over representatives, exercised
by promises and threats relating to the representatives' careers,
is great. This has long been the case; but certain events of recent
years (signal examples are the election of Donald Trump to the
Presidency of the US and Brexit in the UK) ring alarm bells, as
symptoms of failure in a system which has too long relied over-
much on self-imposed restraint and personal principles on the
informal side of the question. This is not the only reason, as the
argument below shows, but it is a major one.

The fallacy in hoping that the people who populate and operate a democracy's institutions will not abuse the latitude for
action they find in them is illustrated by Han Fei's story of the
farmer and the hare. The story is that a farmer was ploughing a
field in the middle of which stood a tree. Suddenly a hare came
racing through the field, collided with the tree, broke its neck
and died. The farmer so enjoyed eating the hare that he thereafter set aside his plough and sat by the tree to wait for another
hare to come along and break its neck. Han Fei, one of the leading Legalist philosophers of the Warring States period in ancient
China (third century BCE), drew the moral: the folly of doing
the same in the hope that another sage king would appear speaks
for itself. His view that government must be a matter of law-
governed institutions rather than the happenstance of talent or
good character in individual people was echoed by Livy two
centuries later.[7]

An appeal to 'constitutional morality' as what politicians will
observe in legislating and governing is therefore no longer good
enough, if it ever was. The formal side of the question has to

address this problem by imposing a far clearer set of requirements on those who occupy the institutions and offices of state.
But because it can never obviate the potential problems that
arise on the informal side, there has to be renewed effort to
create a situation in which the informal side is less susceptible to
the corrosive influences to which, by its very nature, it is
vulnerable.

These are the great questions, both formal and informal,
discussed in the following chapters.

In arguing for the conclusion that the concept of democracy
itself entails a set of specific principles that government must be
based upon, I identify a correlative thesis: that *politics* is too
often the enemy of government – at least, of good government.
Politics is about people organizing themselves to get their policy
preferences enacted; a political party aims to assume the power
of government so that it can further its agenda, which in the
adversarial nature of politics has to be achieved against the
opposition of other parties. Does this way of conducting affairs
lead to good government? If at the minimum democracy means
a state of affairs designed to protect and further the interests *of
the people* – of *all* the people – a surprising requirement comes
into view: that government has to be drained of politics as far as
possible, not in the sense that people should not come together
to argue for a set of policies and a direction of travel for the society and economy, but in the sense that these discussions should
happen on the hustings and when elected representatives form a
government. Once a government is formed its duties to the
people and the national interest must trump party-political
considerations. Politics should assuredly continue outside and
beyond government, but once a government has been installed
on the basis of an agreed platform of policies among the constituent parties forming it, the executive's implementation of them

must be *governmental*, not *party-political*. This simply follows from the idea that democratically constituted government is *for the people* and not *for a winning political party* or *part of the people* – say, the rich, or the working class, or adult males, or the followers of a particular religion.

This view in effect says that in a good state, government transcends politics. This claim will of course be controversial – but only among political activists. I doubt that it would be so controversial among the people as a whole.

Unpacking the concept of democracy does not reveal a perfectibilist possibility.[8] Democracy is about a continual negotiation, a gyroscopic keeping of balance, in an effort to achieve the best for all – not for most or some – and therefore accepting the costs and limitations of inclusivity, of respecting the right of all to participate. Democracy is not an optimal arrangement economically or in terms of ergonomics; it is optimal in human social terms. It is pragmatic in its idealism, recognizing that government cannot do everything, and therefore valorizing civil society activity and organizations and such traditional structures as the family and the community, but at the same time recognizing that the collective endeavour, as expressed through government constituted by the enfranchised to serve their interests collectively and individually, needs to be oriented towards high ideals as the lodestar of its endeavours, even if all recognize the meliorist reality in the perfectibilist hope.

The natural tendency of theorists to position themselves in one of two camps – the conservative and the progressive – too often distorts the analysis they give of what the possibilities are for society. My argument here is that the direction in which the concept of democracy, on analysis, prescriptively points us lies between these positions, though closer to the progressive than the conservative pole. That is not intended to be a *parti pris* point; it is where the argument leads. My own initial starting point is at the progressive pole, but the argument has drawn me at least one step from there by compelling recognition both of the practical and some needed limitations on government – though not of the kind that libertarians (and let there be an emphatic distinction between 'libertarianism' and 'liberalism'[9]) would most like to see in their advocacy of 'small government' and their belief that society is a market in which the mechanisms of 'pricing', whether in economic or social terms, will effect adjustments. The progressive impulse in the inclusivist tendency of democracy finds the human cost, which is to say the moral cost, of an unrestricted market-centred view too high, and will not rest content with it: it demands that the strength of collective power be used where no individual or sectional power is enough to mitigate artificial disadvantages imposed on fellow-citizens, or to address any consequent human suffering when it occurs and however it arises.

In practice much of this is conceded by states which see themselves as democracies. These states see themselves as democracies because they have multiple competing political parties, hold periodic elections by secret ballot to constitute representative government, see peaceful and orderly changes of government as a consequence, have a significant degree of accountability in their institutions, uphold the rule of law, do not have only state-controlled media, and respect the civil liberties of the populace. The states of Europe and North America, together with Australia, New Zealand, Japan, and some others, fill this bill. This is a recent phenomenon in historical terms, and it is a great advance over preceding circumstances – only think of the absolute monarchies, the oligarchies, the disenfranchisement of great majorities of people by those in possession of the various means of power, until the process to remedy this began less than three centuries ago.

But even these states fall short of what the concept of democracy fully entails. Political partisans capture governments as a matter of accepted course, the separate powers of government lie in unseparated hands, the democratic demand for inclusivity is insufficiently met, inequality in the distribution of wealth and social goods is persistently far too great, the conditions for full participation – reliable information, genuinely representative electoral systems, institutional safeguards on probity of performance of servants of the state (including elected representatives) – are not satisfied or are indeed actually violated, and the system falls short in realization of the full extent of rights that democracy *by its nature* defines. While this is so, the major democracies of the advanced world can only be regarded as, at best, partial democracies.

I think everyone who considers the matter knows this. Some aspects of what democracy demands are partially met in these partial democracies, a tacit recognition of the justice of those demands. What our century needs to see everywhere is constitutional reform aimed at bringing democracy fully into operation at last, and capable of remaining apt for the continuing processes of reform that time and changing circumstances will always require. This is because democracy is about people: *the people* – all the people – to whom both state and society belong and for whom they exist.

The first task is to be clear about what *democracy* means. From this all else follows. Accordingly I begin with a detailed explication of this concept in the next chapter.

1

WHAT *DEMOCRACY* ENTAILS

It is an assumption in almost all the world's advanced states that *democracy* is the best – or, in Winston Churchill's phrase, the least bad – of systems for answering the question: What is the source of power and legitimacy of government in a state? The answer variously (and not always synonymously) formulated as 'the people', 'popular will', 'the consent of the people', 'majority will', and cognates, indicates the basic idea, but leaves open the further question of how it is to work. For most of history the word 'democracy' was taken to denote a very undesirable way of sourcing authority in a state, for the reasons given by Plato in the eighth book of his *Republic*: namely, the ignorance, self-interest, short-termism, prejudice, envy, and proneness to rivalry widespread among 'the people'. He thought that democracy would rapidly degenerate into ochlocracy, that is, 'mob rule' or anarchy. A much later sceptic about democracy, the American satirist H. L. Mencken, put the point more succinctly: to believe in democracy, he said, is to believe 'that collective wisdom will emerge from individual ignorance'. And that, in the eyes of sceptics about democracy, is at best; if Plato had been alive in Paris between August 1792 and July 1794 – the Reign of Terror that usurped the French Revolution – he would have seen a paradigmatic and horrifying example of the very worst of his fears about ochlocracy realized.

There is, however, an answer to these sceptical – not to say dismissive and condescending – views, which defends the assumption now widely shared that democracy is indeed the best (or least bad) of systems. A number of significant points have to be taken into that answer, because the idea of democracy involves a dilemma, and solving it is complex. The dilemma of democracy is how to respect two rights that people have, rights that some think are incompatible with each other. On the one hand, there is the right of the people to choose and authorize the government under which they live. On the other hand, there is the people's right to have government performing its functions at least adequately and, one hopes, better than adequately, in the service of their interests.[1] Plato, and two thousand years of theory and practice after him, thought that you could not get from the first of these rights to the second. A defence of democracy must show how this can be done.

Straight away one can state two fundamental reasons why democracy is worth having. First, if what is implied in the idea of democracy is fully realized, it offers the most justifiable basis for legitimacy in government. That is obvious. Only slightly less obvious is the second reason. Few can fail to notice that democracy is an inefficient way of managing a state, given the time and energy consumed in debate, and the disruptive changes in policy, economic direction, and law that can follow changes of government after elections. Tyrannies are greatly more efficient. But the values that are realizable in a democratic order – collected under the label 'civil liberties and human rights' – are a highly significant benefit for which the inefficiency of democracy is a price worth paying.[2]

However, one has to be alert to the fact that a political system's claim to be democratic is not always, or perhaps even often, accurate. Indeed, many democracies in practice tend to be run by hidden oligarchies consisting of whichever group of politicians currently holds power, and by administrators who know how to operate the levers of government in more or less subtle ways. Almost all the world's leading democracies evolved their systems from previous power-holding arrangements, and as a matter of historical record the steps by which this was done were incremental and partial; the degree of control that monarchy or overt oligarchy held was only reluctantly eked away, and those in control of making the change were careful to keep arrangements in place which ensured that their rule or at least influence could still be exercised.[3]

These points tell us that a defence of democracy needs also to be a reassertion of what the very idea of democracy implies, given that inefficiencies of government and the existence of *de facto* oligarchies can, and too often do, blunt or even subvert the point of democracy. In the discussions to follow, a constant theme will be that the concept of democracy itself stipulates what is required for its realization; the concept entails a set of principles which define it, and which if not put into practice render it empty.

This is why specifying the fundamental constitutional and political principles required for a democracy requires an analysis of what is meant by *democracy* itself. It is one of those concepts – in fact, one of those words – that everyone assumes they understand, sometimes without being aware that significantly different interpretations are placed upon it, that democracies can take different forms, and that the vagueness of both word and idea is often exploited for polemical reasons, too often when they do not even remotely apply.

Various forms of democracy exist and have been proposed, but they are taken to share the common assumption, previously noted, loosely describable as a commitment to the principle that 'the people' – which more accurately means 'the enfranchised portion of the people' – by right have a central part to play in conferring legitimacy on the government of the state in which they live. All aspects of this loose characterization – who is enfranchised? what is the part they play? what is the nature and extent of the legitimacy they confer by playing it? – are complex.

The inspiring idea of 'government of the people, by the people, for the people' does not reduce that complexity. When Abraham Lincoln uttered these words in the course of his address at Gettysburg in November 1863, half way through the civil war in America, the franchise in his country was held by white adult male property-owners only. Although the vote was extended to black adult males by the Fifteenth Amendment in 1870, 'Jim Crow' laws in the previously Confederate states effectively kept them out of voting booths until the Civil Rights movement of the 1960s. Note also how long it took for women to be enfranchised. New Zealand women achieved the right to vote in 1893, but in the US and the UK full voting rights were not extended to women on the same basis as men until 1920 and 1928 respectively. It is important therefore to note that the phrase 'the people' has never meant 'the population', and until relatively recently meant only a restricted part of the adult population (depending, moreover, on the definition of 'adult'). The right to vote still excludes many who have other rights and obligations in society that should naturally be accompanied by enfranchisement. For example, in the UK sixteen-year-olds can join the army, can marry, and are already liable to pay tax on earnings above a given threshold, but the voting age is eighteen and was only lowered to eighteen from twenty-one in 1969.

All this said, the trend over the course of the last century has been towards inclusion of greater proportions of the populations of states that have serious ambitions to be described as democratic, which reduces the degree to which invoking 'the people' is an insincere gesture. But it has to be remembered that all franchises are qualified or restricted, and that the phrase 'the people' masks this fact.

The question of the part played by the enfranchised in conferring legitimacy on government is even more complicated. An illustration of this is afforded by an example drawn from the history of the US. In June 1776 the state of Virginia adopted a 'Declaration of Rights', drafted by George Mason, which stated 'That all power is vested in, and consequently derived from, the people'. The Constitution adopted by Virginia just a few weeks later did not reflect this rousing sentiment. It gave the vote only to (white) men of property.[4] Later in that same month of June 1776, with the Virginia Declaration lying before him as he wrote, Thomas Jefferson drafted the 'Declaration of Independence'. It echoes some of the phrases of the Virginia Declaration, phrases which in their turn had been adapted by Mason from John Locke's *Second Treatise on Government* (1689). But the preamble to Jefferson's document contained a significant and deliberate difference. It says that 'Governments are instituted among Men, deriving their just powers from the consent of the governed'. Note the large difference between Mason's words and Jefferson's. The latter substituted a much less committal idea, that of the 'consent' of the governed rather than that of their active grant of permission, which is the implication of Mason's assertion that 'all power is vested in, and consequently derived from, the people'.

Where Mason had thought bottom-up from the enfranchised to what they authorized, Jefferson thought top-down from government to what gave them their authority. The difference is highly significant. In Mason's view the people endow government with legitimacy by the positive step of conferring it. Jefferson's view leaves room for saying that the consent of the governed could be manifested in other ways – by tacit agreement or passive acceptance, for example. The idea that people could 'consent' to being governed merely by not actively opposing government had allowed Locke to say, a century earlier, that England's Parliament 'represented the people' though it was very far from being a democratic institution. Locke allowed himself to say this because the people – here literally meaning the population as a whole – by their compliance and lack of active rejection of government, indicated acceptance of the rule they lived under. The recent English Civil War showed that this acceptance might be withdrawn; so he relied on the assumption that if it is not withdrawn, it is *de facto* granted.[5]

This assumption is of course highly questionable; lack of active refusal or opposition does not license any government to claim that it has the 'consent of the people'. Think of a population divided, weak, and oppressed by force; its lack of resistance is not consent. Think of a population misinformed, misled, lied to; its lack of disagreement is not consent. This implies that the concept of 'consent' is too weak to constitute a ground of authorization for government. It is a necessary condition for that authorization, certainly; but it is not sufficient. Mason's version stated a sufficient condition, Jefferson's version merely a necessary one.

A stronger way of characterizing the role of the enfranchised in Mason's sense is to say that they have 'final authority in the state'. The enfranchised not only confer legitimacy on government, but by the same token specify the nature and limits of its powers, and can recall their authorization. Thus government is both licensed by the enfranchised and answerable to them. In other words again: those appointed to legislate and apply the laws are given *temporary* and *conditional* position only: this way of putting the matter reveals a central feature of the meaning of democracy.

This latter characterization goes a considerable way to capturing the intrinsic meaning of 'democracy', but it is not yet the whole story. In the Introduction it was pointed out that in a democracy every enfranchised person is, by definition, entitled to a vote. It is now accepted that every enfranchised person is entitled to *one* vote; which until quite recently (in fact, until 1948) was not the case in the UK, which had a *plural voting* system (not to be confused with a *plurality voting* system, discussed shortly). The slogan 'one man one vote' was not an idle one in the campaigns for self-determination by colonies of the British Empire after the Second World War. The plural voting system worked like this: all those associated with a university had a vote in their university constituency as well as in their home constituency. All those who owned property which they did not occupy could vote in the constituency or constituencies where their other property lay, as well as in their home constituency. Thus, one person might have several votes if he or she were a member of a university and/or a property owner, thus giving a weighting to more educated and better-off property-owning people.

Part of a justification for plural votes had been offered by John Stuart Mill in his *Considerations on Representative Government*, where, supporting an extension of the franchise to all who could read and write and who paid taxes, he added, 'though everyone [qualified as just described] ought to have a voice, that everyone should have an equal voice is a totally different proposition', for there should be 'some mode of plural voting which may assign

17

to education, as such, the degree of superior influence due to it, and sufficient as a counterpoise to the numerical weight of the least educated class'.[6] This is a view that would resonate with such as Isaac Asimov, who in a much-quoted article entitled 'A Cult of Ignorance' in *Newsweek* in 1980 wrote that democracy promoted the view that 'my ignorance is equal to your knowledge'.[7]

Acceptance of plural voting ended in the UK in 1948, and the assumption now is that every vote has equal weight with every other, because to have a vote is to have a voice, and the most basic assumption of democracy is that no voice has a claim to be louder than any other. But! – in *plurality* ('first-past-the-post' or FPTP) electoral systems, this is not the case. A voter supporting a losing candidate is unrepresented in such a system. Her vote is not equal to the vote of someone who supports a winning candidate; her vote is negated by allowing a mere plurality to decide who shall be elected. The assumption that every vote should have equal weight entails that a voting system *should, in the overall outcome, yield a result as close to proportional to voters' expressed preferences as it can be* (short of allowing minoritarian super-influence on policy, explained below). Both the UK and US electoral systems for the House of Commons and House of Representatives respectively fail this most basic principle of democracy. So do Canada, India, and a significant number of other countries around the world claiming or aspiring to be democracies. Because of their use of the FPTP voting system, none are full democracies.

A simple example demonstrates the undemocratic nature of the FPTP system. Consider a constituency or congressional district of 100 voters, in which 10 candidates stand for election. Suppose 8 of them get 10 votes each, one gets 9 votes, and one gets 11 votes. This last is elected, as having more votes than any

18

other individual candidate – leaving 89 of the 100 voters wholly unrepresented. This distorting system of representation standardly and consistently produces party majorities in legislatures on minorities of the popular vote. Multiply the example just given by (say) 100 constituencies: between them they have 10,000 voters, of whom 1100 voters send 100 representatives to the legislature while the remaining 8900 voters send 0 representatives to the legislature. This is not democracy even on the most tenuous definition in which 'having a vote' is regarded as enough to make a system democratic. Yet this is the situation in all those countries – US, UK, Canada, India, and more – where FPTP is the system in operation.

Systems of proportional representation tend to produce coalition government. There is a strong and highly significant argument that this is desirable in a democracy because of the way it reduces the *political* nature of *government*. I address and explain this crucial point in chapter 3. It relates to the anti-democratic further effect of FPTP voting, which is its entrenchment of two-party systems and correlative exclusion of third and other parties representing other interests in the polity. Having a choice of only two parties, which between them maintain control of a system that refuses to allow the enfranchised anything but a single effective alternative, is arguably undemocratic by itself. It is in practice and effect a version of one-party rule, even if the parties sporadically take turns; for a single party captures the government and, with the artificial majority in the legislature that the FPTP system typically gives, opposition to it is all but powerless.

But it has the yet further deleterious effect of reducing debate about what matters in the state and society to a Manichean 'either-or', each of the opposed sides accusing the other of political evils in public policy matters – taxation, policing, health and education provision, military spending, foreign relations, welfare, social problems, immigration – with resulting simplistic slogan-dominated mutual finger-pointing, losing all the nuance and complexity of issues requiring thoughtful working out and agreement on the best way forward.[8] This latter is what democratic government is meant to provide, and it is what is directly undermined by a political duopoly of rival hostile parties consuming large energies in fighting each other.

The psychological inevitability of this is familiar. Divide things in two and you create a war. From football clubs to referendums the direct confrontation causes people to withdraw to the polarities and the face-to-face stand-off becomes conflictual, even heated and bitter, with people becoming increasingly entrenched and invested in their side of the argument and increasingly reluctant to consider other points of view. This is a deeply injurious and unproductive way of conducting public affairs.

There is a set of standard objections to proportional voting systems, the chief of which I address in Appendix I. The objections to an electoral system that guarantees perpetual two-party politics with the foregoing disadvantages are far more serious.

Observing that an essential component of a democracy is a *proportionately* representational electoral system – one that adequately reflects the diversity of preferences and interests among the enfranchised – leads to another point of equal significance. This is that a democracy is not just a voting system and periodic elections; a set of other conditions require satisfaction also. One is that a democracy cannot consist in simple majoritarianism, given the significance of the principle that government should be constituted to work in the interests of the whole population (see chapter 2) and should be sensitive to the diversity of interests and preferences reflected in the proportionality of the outcome of voting. Respect for civil liberties and human rights, expected as a norm in any polity hoping to be regarded as democratic, specifically includes respect for the rights of minorities, and these have to be entrenched against the majority. But the people of a state likewise need to be protected against minoritarian super-influence on government – that is, very small parties holding the balance of power and forcing their special interests into policy – which certain systems of proportional representation can produce; such therefore need to be avoided.[9]

Behind this point is another that will seem surprising and counter-intuitive to most: that it is highly misleading to reduce the idea of democracy simply to 'rule by the majority'. 'The people' is not an entity, a single thing, with a unitary mind and will. It is a collection of overlapping minorities, or more accurately: it is an aggregation of individuals and minorities. *Majorities* are temporary *coalitions of some set of minorities* coming together over a particular issue. All *rights* are fundamentally individual and minority rights: in their joint application they are the rights not just of this minority or that, not of the majority against the minority, but of the *totality* therefore.

Suppose for a moment that we think, as many standardly do, that 'the majority' is an entity, a kind of corporate person, instead of a shifting and changing coalition of groups of minorities. The widely held view that a majority, thus conceived, has a right to overrule a minority has as its contrapositive the idea that a minority does not have the right to resist or overrule a majority. But this second formulation is not accepted in any democracy, as a defence of minority rights shows; for this defence is that minorities and individuals have rights that the majority must respect and cannot violate. In fact, of course, the principle at work is that any minority (and any individual) has rights that other minorities (or individuals) should not violate; so it is not a matter of a minority overruling a majority at all. But in the fiction of a majority being a corporate entity with a right to have its way in everything just in virtue of being the majority, we see its own repudiation in the implication that no minorities have any rights against it. The concept of democracy itself is a rejection of this implication; and it does so precisely because democracy is about the interests of *all*, not of one section of the populace, however large, or however much it may as a section be more numerous than some other section or sections.

This point – that democracy is not mere majoritarianism – is of great importance. It underlies the necessity, if the state is to be a democratic one, of having a system of representation that will capture the diversity of views and interests among all the enfranchised. It entails that *government*, once formed, must as far as possible *transcend politics* in the sense of transcending political divisions so that it will serve the interests of all and not just a section (however large) which has been successful in capturing the organs of government. Only consider what is standardly the case in so many contemporary polities: a FPTP system hands the levers of power, on a minority of votes cast and an even smaller minority of the population as a whole, to an interest group – a political party – drawn from one minority or set of minorities in the country, which then enacts policies preferred by that group and advantageous to it, and not guaranteed to take the interests of others fully into account – perhaps, indeed, at the expense of certain other minorities in the state. This is how things actually are in Westminster Model polities using the FPTP electoral system. The glaring example is the UK itself.

A majority's being in favour of some course of action is the acceptable means of reaching decisions when no vital interest of a minority is endangered, because it represents the closest approach to consensus in the circumstances. It is a rational means of overcoming what would otherwise be the paralysis of different desires and interests pulling in different directions, if each party to the debate had, when decision is required, equal weight despite unequal representation in the group. In the wisdom that prefers consensus to majority decision, one sees an acceptance that the latter must always leave some minorities unsatisfied or dissenting – inevitable in a pluralistic society, yes, but it demonstrates a falling-short of the democratic ideal that what happens in the polity should be in the interests of all. Consensus of all on a compromise rather than ceding complete dominion to the preference of anything from 51% upwards is better for the quality of democratic life, even if – to repeat an earlier point – it makes for the inefficiency that is an intrinsic but, in respect of civil liberties, highly valuable feature of democracy.

It is worth adding that these reflections show how substantive a point lies in the concept of a 'clear majority' – that is, one that is unequivocal, not within a margin of error, not indicative of fluctuating, uncertain, and marginal, last-minute choices in a vote: this is why a threshold or supermajority bar is the appropriate way to deal with major and highly consequential questions. A vote of 60% or more is an unchallengeable expression of majority preference; whether any smaller percentage would be as conclusive is a matter for debate.

Already one sees that the concept of democracy is a prescriptive one, in virtue of what it means and entails.

The idea at work in these observations is that of a *democratic order*, one in which the interests, rights, and obligations of everyone in the state (not just the enfranchised) are central. At a minimum the rights include freedom of assembly, freedom of expression, freedom of movement, freedom of belief, the rule of law, access to education and economic opportunities, and a free press; and the obligations include abiding by the laws and conventions which have been properly authorized by the enfranchised. These characteristics are necessary for the enfranchised to be the final authority in the state – they could not possess that authority without them – and for the political order in the state to be a democratic one.

Mill's point about ensuring a 'counterpoise to the numerical weight of the least educated class' was intended to address the concern voiced by Plato, that because democracy places power in the hands of people, many of whom are ill-informed, self-interested, prejudiced, envious, and rivalrous, the result will be poor government at best, anarchy at worst.

But these thoughts miss the point of democracy. It is well articulated in a remark made by Colonel Thomas Rainsborough in the English Civil War's Putney Debates of 1647, a discussion among soldiers and officers of the New Model Army of Sir Thomas Fairfax and Oliver Cromwell about constitutional reform. The soldiers of the army, having risked their lives to oppose the absolutist ambitions of the monarchy, desired among other things to see the adoption of universal adult male suffrage, equality before the law, and frequent parliaments. The army's chiefs resisted the suffrage demand, in particular insisting on retaining property qualifications for the right to vote. (They thought that if the unpropertied had the vote they would use it to take away the property of the propertied.) Rainsborough, replying on behalf of the soldiers, memorably said:

> I think that the poorest he that is in England hath a life to live, as the greatest he; and therefore truly, Sir, I think it is clear, that every man that is to live under a government ought first by his

own consent to put himself under that government; and I do think that the poorest man in England is not bound in a strict sense to that government that he hath not had a voice to put himself under.[10]

This remark encapsulates a principle which is central to the idea of democracy. But Plato's strictures alert one to certain other important considerations – in particular, to how the 'dilemma of democracy' is to be resolved. This, recall, is that enfranchisement is by itself no guarantee that it will produce *good* or *good enough* government – what Aristotle called 'sufficient government' – which responds not just to the diversity of interests and demands among the enfranchised, but acts to the overall benefit of all. Accordingly a full extension of the franchise is, as in the case of 'consent', a necessary condition for democracy, but not yet sufficient.

Moreover there are other necessary conditions – necessities, not merely desiderata – of which the two most significant are *secret ballots,* so that voters cannot be forced or otherwise compelled or induced into voting according to someone else's inclinations rather than their own; and the availability of *reliable information* about the state of affairs prevailing in the society and economy, and about candidates' manifestos and commitments in relation to them. Lack of information subverts the point of voters having a choice about how to cast their ballots, and false or misleading information is an indirect form of manipulation and pressure. A necessary condition for democracy to be realized, therefore, is that the act of voting should be *free* and *informed.* This is uncontentious. Arguably, in most contemporary democracies, voting is on the whole free at the ballot box, though the dangers of manipulation and hidden coercion by clever social media campaigns, selectively targeting voters whose psychological triggers have been identified and analysed by 'big data' techniques before they arrive at the ballot box, raises questions. But equally arguably, there is a serious problem about the reliability of the information presented to voters by the Babel of media – and again, not least social media – seeking to influence them. I return to this point below.

Plato's view of the *demos* made him stop short at consideration of the problems he saw in them instead of going on to consider ways in which satisfactory government could be organized on the basis of their participation, even if they were as he described. One finds thinking about this aspect of the matter in Aristotle, and practical methods for bringing popular consent into government among the Romans of the republican era; but the fullest development of democratic theory occurs in the modern period, from the writings of Locke onward.[11] What emerged from the thinking variously of Locke, Montesquieu, Benjamin Constant, Alexis de Tocqueville, John Stuart Mill, and others – and in the theory and practice of the founders of the United States, the laboratory of constitutionalism and a crucial moment in the development of democracy – was a general conception of what Alexander Hamilton named *representative democracy*, in which the two key elements are *representation* itself, and the structure of *institutions and practices* through which representatives carry out the task of government.[12]

The question of institutions and practices is discussed in several of the following chapters. Here it is crucial to consider the concept of *representation*, which contrasts significantly with alternative visions of democracy such as *direct democracy* – by frequent referendums, or the actual presence of the enfranchised in decision-making processes – or *sortition*, in which members of the legislative body are appointed by lottery, or *cellular* or *associationist democracy*, in which (for a chief example) local democratically elected bodies appoint representatives to regional bodies which in turn appoint representatives to national bodies; or *deliberative democracy*, of which there are numerous versions, most (other than *elite deliberative democracy*) predicated on a rejection of Platonic scepticism about the chance of sufficient government emerging from unmediated popular action.

The first version – direct democracy – is not representative because it does not require to be so; the second – sortition – is randomly so; the third – cellular – involves a highly indirect form of representation. The first and second invite Platonic scepticism about the degree of informedness, altruism, and long-termism that would be manifested by legislatures thus formed, characteristics that would seem to be required for the operation of both sufficient and efficient government. In reply, proponents of direct democracy appeal to the wisdom of the masses, while proponents of sortition argue that a randomly chosen legislative body would not perform much worse than a set of career politicians, and might perform better – especially if, as with juries, appointment were for a set term so that participants would have no vested interest in doing anything other than using their best endeavours, having no career ambitions or party-political pressures acting on them. The third suggestion attenuates the connection between the enfranchised and government far more than the familiar systems of representation in most contemporary democracies, and it attracts scepticism accordingly. Some of the points at stake here, especially those relating to the first two alternative versions of democracy, together with variants of 'deliberative democracy', are important and are taken up and discussed in Appendix II.

In a representative democracy voters choose people to serve in the legislature on their behalf, not as delegates or messengers merely conveying the various sentiments, or perhaps just the majority sentiment, of their voters, but as plenipotentiaries – that is, possessors of full and independent powers – to investigate, get facts, listen to expert advice, discuss and debate, and on this basis to form a judgment and to act in the best interests of both constituents and country. If they do not do a good job on the electors' behalf, the electors can expel them. That is the paradigm. It is famously expressed in an address to the electors of the city of Bristol by their Member of Parliament, Edmund Burke, in 1774:

> Certainly, gentlemen, it ought to be the happiness and glory of a representative to live in the strictest union, the closest correspondence, and the most unreserved communication with his constituents. Their wishes ought to have great weight with him; their opinion, high respect; their business, unremitted attention. It is his duty to sacrifice his repose, his pleasures, his satisfactions, to theirs; and above all, ever, and in all cases, to prefer their interest to his own. But his unbiased opinion, his mature judgment, his enlightened conscience, he ought not to sacrifice to you, to any man, or to any set of men living . . . Your representative owes you, not his industry only, but his judgment; and he betrays, instead of serving you, if he sacrifices it to your opinion . . . government and legislation are matters of reason and judgment, and not of inclination; and what sort of reason is that, in which the determination precedes the discussion . . . parliament is a deliberative assembly of one nation, with one interest, that of the whole; where, not local purposes, not local prejudices, ought to guide, but the general good, resulting from the general reason of the whole. You choose a member indeed; but when you have chosen him, he is not member of Bristol, but he is a member of parliament.[13]

28

The point of this is precisely that 'government and legislation are matters of reason and judgment' and therefore representatives are tasked with acquiring relevant information and applying consideration to it. The concept of representation answers Plato's concerns; but not only this, the key further element is that the enfranchised not only appoint representatives but dismiss them if they do not perform their task well. The enfranchised's power of appointment and dismissal is the key feature of democracy; representation is a temporary office; in this lies the authority of the people over government.

When a representative democracy resorts to referendums to resolve questions, it is an abdication of what representative democracy is for, namely, to resolve the dilemma of democracy by getting from the right of the people to a voice to the right of people to sufficient ('good enough') government, this latter to be achieved by parlaying the preferences expressed by the enfranchised into an organized administration of endeavours to meet them in the best interests of all. When representatives duck their responsibility to do this, choosing to hold a referendum because they cannot do what they are elected and employed to do, namely, reach a considered decision, they are abandoning the democratic process to the first of those rights alone, the one that can and too often does subvert the second right.

A point not yet sufficiently made concerns who should be enfranchised in a democracy. This question might more illuminatingly be put by asking: Who should be excluded from the franchise, and why? Looked at from this angle, the answer is clear enough. It is that all should be enfranchised who, provided that they have reached an age at which they can reasonably be supposed capable of understanding the general issues at stake and forming preferences concerning them, have a material interest in the outcome of an election or referendum. It is not arbitrary to suggest that this age should be sixteen, given the consensus on the view that from this age onward individuals can assume other responsibilities of adulthood such as military service, marriage, and employment.

The franchise should be as inclusive and extensive as possible, indeed as close to being coterminous with the population – hence, 'the people' truly meant – as it can be, subject only to the question of capacity to understand what is at issue in a vote. Giving the franchise to people aged sixteen years and above achieves this desideratum. Certain other exclusions from the franchise might be argued for – in the UK members of the House of Lords cannot vote, because doing so would amount in effect to their having a double vote, and in some countries people serving custodial sentences have their right to vote suspended until their prison term is over.[14] But exclusions need to be justified case by case; the presumption must be that 'the people' means as many of the people as possible.

There is a further point about the power of recall that the enfranchised have over those they elect as representatives. What gives effect to this is that elections have to be held periodically, with an outer limit to the length of time that can elapse between elections, and with no power in a government to extend its tenure indefinitely. The question therefore arises of how long the longest permissible period between elections should be. In New Zealand elections are required by law every three years; a much-voiced criticism is that this is too short a period for legislation to be well prepared and debated.[15] In the US elections for the House of Representatives occur every two years. This means that representatives devote a significant proportion of their time and energy to perpetual fund-raising and campaigning, having to start over for the next election immediately upon winning the one just past. A period of either four or five years, and certainly no longer than the latter, has achieved the status of norm in most democratic polities, and a defensible case can be made for either. A legislature's mandate needs always to be reasonably fresh, and that applies even more emphatically to a government. Five years would seem to be the outer limit beyond which a mandate can no longer be securely claimed.

Let us return for a moment to the kinds of general definition of democracy that tend to serve for most unanalytic purposes. The misleading notion of 'majority rule' has been mentioned already. Another chief example is that a democracy is a political order characterized by 'free and fair elections' and 'a free press (or media)'. This is true as far as it goes, but it does not go very far. It has already been noted that the demand for *fair* elections is not met by unrepresentative electoral systems. Now one can add that mere absence of coercion at a polling station is not enough for voting to be *free*, for if voters are not properly informed, or – worse – are actively misinformed, their choices are not free; so this freedom is connected with the freedom of the media, and the nature of their behaviour. Are the media free? It is not enough that media of news and opinion are not censored or controlled by authorities in power, for where media are owned by individuals with agendas of their own, and/or where they are obliged by commercial pressures constantly to stimulate the attention of readers by partisanship, exaggeration, and a variety of distractions, they are in fact simultaneously anarchic and constrained, and both in the worst senses. Above all, the advent of the phenomenon of 'social media' has weaponized all that is worst about propaganda, misinformation, deliberate falsehood, manipulation, and interference, including interference in a state's affairs by other states. Cyberspace is the agora of an ochlocracy even more than it is the forum of a positively good

31

global democracy of debate: the bad always drives out the good in all things, and social media is a vivid case in point.

Use of the words 'free' and 'fair' in 'free and fair elections' and 'a free media' is accordingly far from unproblematic.

It is pertinent to note, at this juncture, a remark by the political philosopher Ian Shapiro, that whereas the idea of democracy is 'nonnegotiable' in polities that regard themselves as democracies, among political theorists there is considerable scepticism about its value.[16] The scepticism ranges from Plato's views about the competency of 'the people' to exercise political authority, through Rousseau's belief that democracy can only work in very small village-like communities, to John Dunn's view that it has never been convincingly explained how the utopian aspirations of participatory democracy are to be achieved. Indeed, Dunn argued that democracy's sustainability depended not on its intrinsic merits as a system, but on a successful economy and the existence of a flourishing middle class. In the absence of these factors, he argued, democracy is reversible.[17]

Shapiro observes that democracy has come to be viewed as, in essence, merely a matter of competition for the majority's vote – a reductive, aggregative view. His own view is that democracy is a system for minimizing 'domination' of the populace by those in authority, defining 'domination' as 'illegitimate exercise of power' and observing that 'hierarchical relations . . . always [contain] the possibility that, left unchecked, they can facilitate domination.'[18]

The concept of representative democracy constitutes a large part of the answer to the scepticism Shapiro notes. His point about democratic arrangements constituting a barrier against domination is a good one, though it cannot be the whole story. Most certainly, a democratic order has to be one in which the nature and extent of the powers of government, as licensed by the enfranchised, must be defined, and violations of their limits controlled. Democratic arrangements need to be *constitutional* in this sense. But a democracy is not only about imposing limits on governmental power; as an order intended to benefit those who constitute and assent to it, considerably more is required. Much of what is discussed in the coming chapters turns on this and associated points.

The foregoing is not yet, by far, a complete account of what principles a democracy worthy of the name should rest upon, but it is appropriate to sum up the points so far made. They are that a democracy requires a proportional system of voting by secret ballot which produces a result as close to the overall variety of voter preferences as possible without giving a distorting degree of influence to very small groups; the fullest possible extension of the franchise and certainly from the age of sixteen; periodic elections no longer than, at the utmost, five years apart; and constitutional entrenchment of individual and minority rights. These points can hardly be contentious. The idea that those elected should be representatives rather than mandatories of the enfranchised, charged with an express duty to get information, debate, consider, and judge what it is in the best interests of the country *as a whole* and *all* its people in the matter of policies and laws, is designed to meet the dilemma of democracy, that is, how to get from the right of the enfranchised to a voice to their right to good-enough government. This point might be contested by defenders of direct, sortitive, and deliberative democracy, considerations to which I recur below in defence of the idea – one that first emerged from the theory and the practice of democracy-making between Locke and Mill and the founding of the United States in between – of representative democracy.

From this summary of principles so far identified, a definition of the term 'democracy' offers itself as denoting the order of affairs in a polity in which the enfranchised, consisting of all the population except those too young to be expected to understand the issues at stake, set up a government and explicitly endow it with authority to act in the interests of all, doing so in a way that takes account of the range and variety of interests and preferences among the enfranchised. To modify a relevant catchphrase: democratic government is government *for the people* on terms set, and authority given, *by the people.*

How do the world's leading democracies fare in the light of this first raft of principles? As noted, a number of them fall at the very first hurdle because of their undemocratic electoral systems – and, it might now also be added, the restrictive age qualification of their franchises. But alas, these are not the only problems, and the ideal of democracy is not yet fully in view. In the next chapters these further problems will appear, illustrating the principles which, if applied, would remedy them and enable democracy to be as the concept itself entails that it should be. The tenor of the entire case to be made is that democracy is the means to achieve the desideratum of government that serves the people – all the people – by 'transcending politics' in a sense that the chapters that follow demonstrate.

2

THE PURPOSE
OF GOVERNMENT

The second point to be addressed is this fundamental question: What is government for? More to the point: In a democracy, what is government for?

James Madison, George Mason, and others assembled in Williamsburg in the spring of 1776 to begin drafting a constitution. The preamble to it said:

> Government is or ought to be instituted for the common benefit, protection, and security of the people, nation or community. Of all the various modes and forms of government, that is best which is capable of producing the greatest degree of happiness and safety and is most effectually secured against the danger of maladministration; and that when any government shall be found inadequate or contrary to these purposes, a majority of the community hath an indubitable, unalienable, and indefeasible right to reform, alter, or abolish it, in such manner as shall be judged most conducive to the public weal.

The arguments of the Founders about the right to resist bad government were, of course, directed at the British Crown; it was the rhetoric of the revolution. Invocations of 'the people' and its rights did not include slaves or women; 'the people' were adult white men only. What has, with regret, to be acknowledged as the hypocrisy of the constitution persisted until the 1960s.

But the wording of the draft preamble is suggestive. It offers at least part of an answer to the question: Why do the people constitute a government? Evidently a generalized version of the preamble indicates that the purpose of government is to serve the people's interests. What are the people's interests, in the required general sense?

One thing immediately clear is that a collective is stronger than the strongest individual in it – or should be. To protect the weak against the depredations of the strong, to promote fairness and security, to succour the ones who fall by the wayside, to work to make life better and to make it good, are tasks that a collective can take on for the benefit of its members. Given the inclusivity presupposed to the notion of 'the people', it would seem that the purpose of democratic government is in good part captured by these thoughts.

Note that when Locke and other early theorists of politics talk of the provision of 'security' as a reason for government they mean predictability, the opposite of the uncertainties of the exercise of arbitrary power. Locke talks of 'standing rules', 'declared laws', 'settled standing laws', 'stated rules of right and property', 'promulgated, established laws, not to be varied', all targeted at the idea, put forward by the defender of absolute monarchy Sir Robert Filmer, that decisions are always, in the end, made at someone's personal discretion, and that such discretion might be whimsical or arbitrary. Locke was fiercely opposed to this. To be subject to the 'inconstant, uncertain, unknown will of another man' was the negation of liberty – the condition of a slave. Locke objected to Hobbes' solution to the uncertainties of the state of nature by saying that it was pointless to escape the 'pole-cats and foxes' there only to fall under the dominion of a lion. This is an excellent point.

To identify democracy as the political order predicated on the interests and participation *of all* already says much about what the aim of *democratic government* must be. But though this is right, it is not yet specific enough for our purposes. For example, what does this mean in practice for the great and perennial dilemma of political philosophy: How to achieve the joint realization of freedom and fairness in society? Privileging one of these desiderata seems to necessitate diminishing the other. If people are left free to satisfy their ambitions, society becomes unfair, even when efforts are made to equalize opportunities: for inequality of talents in a domain of equal opportunities will rapidly result in unequal outcomes. But efforts to ensure fairness, by restraining some and discriminating positively in favour of others, among other things redistributing the fruits harvested by the successful to the less successful, interferes with freedom. As Isaiah Berlin thought, liberty and equality appear to be irresolvable contra-dictions, leading pessimists to conclude that the efforts made by a society to achieve both must inevitably fail, at best result-ing in a constant and unsteady negotiation in which first one then the other is emphasized. In practice, as the history of the advanced economies shows, it is liberty that most usually dominates, and in societies where compulsion is used to impose greater degrees of equality, economic failure has so far been the outcome.[1]

Consider what is at stake. A government seeking to optimize the circumstances of all would hear, on the one hand, warnings that if an increasing imbalance of wealth occurs in society, and with it its usual correlative of an imbalance of power, then the aims of democracy will be undermined, because money-power in a society represents, in effect, a form of plural voting: wealthy interests have a far louder voice – an amplified, multiplied voice – in the public square than the individuals or collectives of individuals seeking to maintain their rights. The outcome of the process is that the very rich few gain and thereafter maintain control over a system that perpetuates their tenure of privilege at the expense of the many.

At the same time this government will hear that an effort to take redistributive control of wealth in effect simply displaces that power from the hands of businessmen to the hands of bureaucrats, and that it is a fallacy to think that a polity run by bureaucrats will invariably be more benign than one controlled by businessmen. Such sceptics will say that a Central Committee system whose experience of seeking to benefit the many might have made it less sympathetic to the recalcitrant material of which the many are made, might be a worse option than a plutocrat–helot society, because at least in this latter some – the plutocrats – are free, while in the former all are helots. And, the sceptics will then add, in the latter system there is always a chance for the helots that they might become plutocrats themselves, while in the former there is none.

So far, then, we have available the idea that the aim of constituting a society is to escape both the 'polecats and foxes' on one side and the 'lion' on the other, and to find a way of resolving the tension between the freedom and the fairness from which most people jointly wish to benefit. This, note, is the *society* which, at the minimum – and the minimum is not enough – we require. It must point us in the direction of what we therefore require of *government*.

What, then, are the purposes of government in a democracy? An answer has to be better than an answer merely to the more general and prior question, 'What is government for?' Anarchy has its proponents, and if a case for government is to be more persuasive than the case for anarchy, it has to turn on the merits of answers to that prior question; but they would not yet constitute an answer to the question specifically about the purposes of democratic government.

For the purposes of the modern debate the chief examples of answers to this question were offered, in the seventeenth and eighteenth centuries, by Hobbes, Locke, Rousseau, and Kant, in the nineteenth century by Mill, and in the twentieth century by John Rawls and his followers and critics. With the exception of Mill, these thinkers suggested their answers indirectly, in the course of providing an account of how organized society arises out of preceding conditions, either of primitive anarchy – a 'state of nature' – or in Rawls' version an idealized 'original position' in which people who are about to constitute a society decide how they would like it to be organized.[2]

The views of the two seventeenth-century thinkers named were seminal, in proposing a *contractarian* thesis about the basis of political society. In essence the view is that because the state of nature is, as Hobbes argued, dangerous and insecure, or as Locke more mildly put it, attended with 'inconveniences' – primarily the 'inconvenience' of each individual having to defend or enforce the natural rights he or she possesses – people agreed to come together in a mutual contract to yield up all (Hobbes) or some (Locke) of their personal liberty in return for the protection of the society constituted by their mutual contract. Fundamentally, therefore, government is for protection of the people: public order, defence, security, and (for Locke in particular, an important point) safe tenure of property.

For Rawls an implied chief purpose of government is to ensure a distribution of social and economic goods that is as advantageous as it can be for the least well placed in society, the aim being to render the society maximally *fair*. He takes it as read that government has other functions, public order and security among them.[3] His version of the seminal contract is the agreement reached in the 'original position' over the nature of the distributions to be made.

The notion of a contract is of course an explanatory fiction, but insofar as it implies an answer to the question under consideration it is a useful starting point. In Locke the implication of the contract is that government is limited to providing security and protection – that is, order and the institution and enforcement of law, and defence against enemies internal and external. In Hobbes the contract creates an absolute sovereign power whose duty is to protect the contracting parties' lives, in the process establishing judiciaries, making laws about property, and deciding on peace and war.[4] Hobbes' absolute sovereign, whether a person or a body of men, is not itself a party to the contract, and its creation by the contract is irreversible and unchallengeable – except in the single case of failure to protect the contracting parties' lives, in which case the people will be justified in overthrowing it. In Locke the state is not absolute in power, for it is limited to the duty specified in the contract, and must otherwise leave individual rights untrammelled. If it invades people's rights and fails to act in their best interests, the people have a right to overthrow it.[5] In specifying protection as the essential purpose of government these early forms of contractarian theory anticipate more recent arguments in favour of 'Night Watchman' minimalist theories of the state, an example of which is offered by Robert Nozick in his *Anarchy, State and Utopia* (1974).[6] Mill gives a perfect encapsulation of such a view when he writes: 'Security of person and property, and equal justice between individuals, are the first needs of society, and the primary ends of government: if these things can be left to any responsibility below the highest, there is nothing, except war and treaties, which requires a general government at all.'[7]

Although obviously significant, and a central component of what government is for, is 'providing protection' the whole story of the purpose of government?

A complication in the early discussion of this question is that writers on the subject did not regularly distinguish between *society* and *the state*, and were therefore apt to conflate questions about the advantages of society – that is, living in general harmony with and alongside others for such reasons as companionship, pooling of resources, and mutual assistance – and the advantages of a state – that is, organization, defence against bad people within and enemies without, the administration of justice, and more. The point is an important one because the contract hypothesized in the contractarian theory institutes a *state* not a society, and relates to the public aspects of communal life, leaving its private aspects largely out of account. This has some problematic consequences. Because – for a chief example – the contributions of women in so many societies are made in the private sphere, and indeed are often expressly relegated to that sphere, they are only parties to the contract indirectly through their relationship with men. By the same token full participation in such a contract is not possessed by slaves, minorities, and others who have been denied full (or any) citizenship status in various societies at different times in history. The contractarian theorists had a particular image in mind of the lives and activities of parties to the contract, and failed to recognize the implications of its being a picture of the lives and activities of the enfranchised only – and male ones at that.[8]

While recognizing the distinction between asking 'What is government for?' and 'Why do human beings gather together into communities and societies?' it is of equal or greater importance to recognize that some of the advantages of society are enhanced or even indeed only made possible by the existence of government. This is a fundamental fact about humans as social beings, prefigured in the fact that other kinds of social animals have organizing structures in their communities – the dominance of the alpha male baboon, the leadership of the matriarchal elephant – with consequent advantages to all in the troop or herd. In exploring the purposes of government one has to take account of its actual and possible social aims and effects also; the minimalist 'Night Watchman' view neglects this dimension entirely.

This, of course, in its turn reminds one of the inescapable fact that views about the purposes of government always rub against *political* views about what a government at a time and place ought to be doing or not doing in light of the political debate locally in progress. The challenge of disentangling the theoretical concept of 'the purposes of government' from such debate is significant. But it is a challenge worth trying to meet: for it is arguably the case that it is a matter of principle that *certain fundamental purposes of government should be resistant to the vagaries of historically parochial political conflict*. In this and later chapters this is a key point.

The answer to the question, 'What is government for?' in the case of tyrannies and oligarchies is clear: the tyrant is interested in power, in getting it and keeping it, and if tyrannical power is exercised with cruelty and oppression, the tyrant's tenure of power will also be aimed at his own self-preservation against the resentment of the oppressed. If by 'oligarchy' one means cooperating members of a class, group, or organization, who between them hold the levers of power – for respective examples: an aristocracy, wealthy people, a dominant religion, a political faction – then the purpose of government is to protect and enhance the interests of that group or faction.

In systems that regularly produce two-party politics, with possession of the reins of government alternating sporadically between the parties, government is for the enactment of the policies favoured by one of the parties. Put thus baldly, political systems – especially those with FPTP electoral systems which inevitably produce two-party arrangements – are indistinguishable from oligarchies; indeed, they *are* oligarchies in effect; the oligarchy of the party that wins control of government.

Such views about the purposes of government are informative because they indicate, by contrast, what a rational and disinterested view of the fundamental purpose of government might be. It would not be for keeping an individual or faction in power, nor for ensuring the benefit of that individual or faction at the expense of others, nor for imposing certain views or ways of life on others or denying them their different views or lifestyles. Instead it implies that government requires to have a conception of the interests of all, of equal concern for all, and of a just balance in the distribution of opportunities and access to social goods. If these desiderata are couched in the language of 'protection' as in Locke and others, they would be formulated as protecting the interests of all members of society against the depredations, the overweening or distorting influence, the non-benign self-interest, of others within and outside the society in question.

This formulation is acceptable, but in being phrased in terms of what it prevents it says nothing about what it promotes. So the same considerations suggest a positive version in which acting to ensure equal concern and respect for all, and enablement of access to social goods of health, education, and welfare, constitute aims that serve the interests of all. 'Equal concern' implies equality before the law, protection of rights and civil liberties, provision of social infrastructure (e.g. health and education), and the protections and remedies of a system of justice.

The employment of the phrase 'equal concern' here borrows from the distinction drawn by Ronald Dworkin between *treating people as equals*, that is, 'with equal concern and respect', and *treating them equally*. This latter can be unjust: suppose you impose a diet of 3000 calories a day on both an athlete needing 5000 calories a day and an elderly lady needing 2000 calories a day. You are treating them both equally, but each unfairly.[9] By contrast, 'equal concern' means not discriminating in adverse ways, but with equally positive regard to individual rights and circumstances.

There can be, and has been, political debate about some and even most of this palette of purposes for government. Here is a very different view, propounded by a former mayor of Kansas City, Missouri: 'Government in a democracy is essentially a conservative institution. It is responsible for creating and sustaining markets, enforcing contracts, protecting private property, and producing systems of education and infrastructure that allow commerce to function efficiently.'[10] This is a familiar view of 'small government' advocates who see anything beyond this strictly banausic provision as unjustified, not least because it requires tax dollars for programmes with which they vehemently disagree. And indeed many regard it as reasonable to expect a consensus that, independently of party-political views about how the following desiderata are to be achieved, government has among its purposes the pursuit of several economic aims, among them promoting economic growth because this raises the populace's living standards and makes resources available for national investment in physical and social infrastructure. Likewise seeking full employment, price stability and control of inflation, and an advantageous balance of payments, would be regarded by many as rational and uncontentious aims. Those who disagree are primarily concerned with the sustainability and environmental impact of economic activity; the relentless pursuit of economic growth, and the associated relentless cajoling of people to consume more and more because consumption is the driver of economic success, has proved extremely damaging to the natural environment.

Politics enters the picture with debates about how these matters are to be treated, which involves questions about the nature and levels of taxation and spending, and income redistribution. But again, one can ask whether meeting the economic aims of government is the whole story. How they are realized in practice is not a neutral matter. They can be realized in more and less unjust ways, in ways that include or exclude more sections of society, in ways that sequester a far larger proportion of benefits to a small number of people.[11] These are functions of political choice – but the concept of democracy places a limit of principle on such choices: not all political choices are equally justifiable in a democracy, because the concept of democracy entails the concept of the participation of the people as a function of their entitlement to equal concern; which in turn entails that the system not be loaded against some – and certainly not the majority – in favour of those who at any point in time have their hands on the levers of political and economic influence.

This is a simple corollary of the fact that democracy entails fair participation and fair opportunity. It does not entail equality, but it entails respect for considerations of social justice. It is certainly inconsistent with a system that *creates* poverty on purpose to generate wealth for one group; but it also raises questions about any system of distribution of opportunity, participation, and wealth itself, that even by neutral operation of its mechanisms results in disproportions so great that in the same society there can be people living in conspicuous luxury while others sleep on the street. Whereas there is no justification for placing a cap on what anyone might earn or accumulate by their endeavours or talents, providing they are legally exercised, there can equally be no justification for not ensuring that certain minimum standards are observed in providing a safety net for people unable to provide for themselves. A society which allows no one to be without accommodation, sustenance, and opportunities to escape dependency where possible, will of course have to pay the cost of free riders; but to determine policy on the basis of avoiding the latter guarantees that the minimum standards just described will not be met.

The question of democratic principle at stake here concerns the application of equal concern and the right to participate. To participate in what? The freedoms and opportunities that a democratic order makes possible, and thereafter protects, cannot operate as if their operation were only possible on condition that some in society suffer so that others can benefit, or on condition that some in society are denied those freedoms and opportunities in practice by the resulting distribution. All the enfranchised by definition have the right – and, arguably, duty – to constitute and authorize government to act both in their interests and in those of the unenfranchised; that is, for everyone. It would be irrational for denizens of an 'original position' to conclude that a condition of the opportunity for some to be extremely wealthy should be that some suffer immiseration.[12] It is in the interests of all that, even if there is no ceiling on how economically successful some can be, there should be a floor below which no one can fall.

There is, in fact, an implicit consensus in most advanced democratic societies to this effect, though it is not seen as an entailment of *democracy* that this should be so, but rather as an entailment of a conception of *civilized values*. It is most certainly that, but the interesting point is that the latter are themselves correlative with *democratic values*, and the logical connection lies in the idea of inclusiveness as implied in that of 'the people', and the idea of a minimum acceptable distribution among the people dictated by considerations of humanity as implied by 'civilized values'. There is a virtuous conceptual circle here. Whereas it is possible to imagine a non-democratic dispensation in which civilized values obtain, it is not possible to imagine a democracy in which civilized values are regarded as unnecessary or merely optional.

More contentious still, however, are arguments for aims of government which rise above the pragmatic – if we allow that basic welfare provision can be regarded as a pragmatic consideration. In classical antiquity a trope of discussion about the good *polis* or city state – for example, in Aristotle – is that it exists not just so that its citizens can live, but so that they can live 'nobly'. One recalls that in Aristotle's day 'citizens' meant a minority of inhabitants of a *polis*, and exclusively the male citizens at that. When Aristotle's political writings were recovered in the Renaissance they were welcomed by the thinkers of the Italian city states, for whom the purpose of good government was promotion of the honour of the state in art, learning, and the elegances of life, ideals promoted by Petrarch and Leonardo Bruni among others. Once again, though, the beneficiaries were not likely to extend beyond the better-placed of the citizens.[13]

Hyperbolic as the idea of promoting 'noble lives' may seem, the ideals connoted in it are resonant. Of course, they would not resonate with the advocates of 'small government' for whom 'noble lives' are matters for private achievement, not public provision. Even here there is a tension, however: public support for the arts finds justifiers among some on the right of politics. Moreover the philanthropy of the rich, when it occurs, is typically exercised for public benefit, which is welcome, but paradoxical: if the public benefit matters – even if more modestly construed as the general opportunity for 'good lives' rather than noble ones – then a system that distributes wealth in highly disproportionate ways, leaving the public benefit to be met by individual whim, is problematic.

Given the contentious nature of counting 'promoting noble lives' – lives touched and enhanced by general education (not just vocational training) and the enjoyment of the arts, culture, and constructive leisure – among the purposes of government, one can concessively (in accepting the realities) suggest that government does well if it at least encourages the promotion of the opportunities for such lives, for example by providing tax breaks for philanthropic support of the arts. If it did not go that far, it might at very least not stand in the way of efforts to promote noble lives, if this is not just a disguise for some sectarian or factional purpose. This again identifies the crux point at which the question arises: When does discussing the purposes of government become a political debate?

The Preamble to the US Constitution, thought to have been written by Gouverneur Morris, who at any rate vigorously supported its inclusion in the document, states, by way of explaining what the Constitution is for, that the purpose of government is to 'establish Justice, insure domestic Tranquility, provide for the common Defence, promote the general Welfare, and secure the Blessings of Liberty to ourselves and our Posterity.' This can be read minimalistically as a 'Night Watchman' view, or a more ambitious reading can be given of the first and fourth conjuncts: 'establish Justice . . . promote the general Welfare'. If 'establishing justice' includes economic and social justice, and if the 'general welfare' is promoted by provision of education, health services, and support for cultural life and amenity, then the purpose of government is actively to ensure space for its promotion in diverse ways by citizens themselves. Putting matters like this avoids what would be a legitimate criticism, namely, that 'a government' would know best what promotes a good life and society. On the other hand, if this notion relates only to protecting individuals from interference with their own private efforts at securing health, education, and a good life, then they are the basis for the long-prevailing American minimalist view. Such a view would not accept that a society should pool and redistribute resources for the society's various efforts at making good lives possible.

Here again is where politics cuts across the question of the purposes of government. The twentieth century saw many developed states increasing the reach of government involvement in aspects of life that would have been unthinkable in the preceding century, and which greatly trouble those with libertarian instincts. Criminalization of supply and use of heroin, cocaine, marijuana, and similar substances, bans on smoking in public places, and the legal requirement to use seatbelts in motor vehicles and crash-helmets on motorbikes are examples of state control of private activity. The list can be expanded a long way. Certain of these interventions can be justified on economic grounds: the burden on the health services is reduced if greater safety precautions are taken to reduce levels of injury in road traffic accidents – speed limits are a case in point, and the complexity of medical treatment of individuals injured in serious traffic accidents absorbs a great deal of time and expense that, say, a motorbike helmet could have prevented – to say nothing of the benefit to the individual herself.

But not all these interventions have such justification. Some are straightforwardly illogical – and, incidentally, extremely expensive to implement; and cause greater problems than they purport to address – and at the same time are a major invasion of privacy. Drug policies are the classic example. Some dangerous substances, such as alcohol and nicotine, are legal but their supply and use are managed, whereas others (some, like marijuana, arguably less harmful than these) are proscribed, with large amounts of policing time and expense thereby incurred and major entrepreneurial opportunities for crime thereby created. The policies are almost wholly ineffective because people who want access to these substances get them. The example of efforts to control alcohol use is instructive: alcohol causes harm to some, but is used with reasonable good sense by most, the controls on supply and use are likewise largely sensible, and sanctions for abuse (driving while over a safe limit of consumption, for example) are fairly effective. 'Prohibition' in the US in the 1920s exemplifies everything that needs to be said on the point: it criminalized most of the population, did not expunge alcohol use from society but hugely inflated opportunities for criminal organizations, and was a failure. The same is true of drug policy now. The motivation for it is neither logical nor economic but moral – that is, it reflects the moral disapproval that 'Temperance' movements of the nineteenth century succeeded in normalizing in society and extending to other types of substances besides alcohol. Opium was a legally purchasable substance in pharmacies in Britain until the First World War; there is no evidence that its free availability for several centuries beforehand caused social collapse and mayhem. (Somewhat to the contrary, so someone of a sardonic turn of mind might point out, its free availability coincided with the height of Empire.)

Still, questions of the limits of state intervention in matters of private life and choice remain questions of politics and morality, and of the nature and justification of individual rights. These are enormously important questions, but how they are to be answered cannot be deduced from democratic principles alone, beyond the constraints that it is not for a powerful minority – a self-interest group like a religious movement, say – to impose public policy that has no justification other than its own moral preferences.

Two thoughts need to be set alongside the observation that since the first half of the twentieth century governments have intervened increasingly in private lives, becoming 'nanny states' telling us what is good and bad for us and obliging us to act according to their instructions. One is that in the same period conceptions of civil liberties and human rights have become salient in national and international discourse, not yet sufficiently effective in stopping atrocities, but in developed states they have significant effect. There is doubtless a mutual influence at work between increasing state intervention and increasing insistence on individual liberties, as society has a conversation with itself about how it wishes to arrange matters in various respects. But – and this is the second thought – this situation represents a huge advance over the one that so long prevailed, in which monarchs and prelates forced much greater control over individuals, with much harsher sanctions, than would be tolerated now. Compulsory church-going and tithe-giving, the death sentence for not believing what you are told to believe, harshly punitive control of the expression of individuals' sexuality and affections if they did not conform to a norm laid down by the authorities – these are examples of how more enlightened attitudes have to a large extent liberated people in some parts of the world – not in all: mainly, in the more democratic parts of the world: a speaking fact.

J. K. Galbraith observed that considerations about the line of demarcation between public and private spheres lead to a crucial point: that it is arguably a vital purpose of government in a democracy to referee imbalances of private influence and power in the economy, society, and political order.[14] The point has become a familiar one in a new guise: despite the belief that markets will always tend to equilibrium through the price mechanism, the practical tendency is for concentrations of power and resource to accumulate, resulting in the growth of ever-larger corporations. This stimulates the growth of other large corporations in competition; large corporations wield political power through donations and – eventually – by becoming 'too big to fail'; labour organizes to oppose the power of corporations; the dynamic of tension and perhaps conflict and destabilization unfolds, with the individual caught in the middle. It ought to be a purpose of any government to ensure that the operation of such imbalances does not crush individuals and minorities. In *democratic* government this duty lies at the centre of its *raison d'être*.

The foregoing considerations merely sample the kinds of point that need discussion in answering the question, 'What does the concept of democracy itself suggest regarding the purposes of government?' But to gain traction on the point for present purposes, we can ask this: Does the concept of democracy itself help to choose between the minimalist view and a more ambitious one? Is there anything implicit in the concept of democracy that suggests that the purpose of government is to realize a conception of a good life and society, as something more than merely providing protection for the liberty and property of individuals?

The beginnings of an answer lie in the answer to another question: In what circumstances can a government in a democracy require of the people that they accept being made poorer, accept restrictions on their civil liberties, and accept being put at risk of their lives? The answer is: in a dire emergency such as war. Absent a dire emergency, a government in a democracy would be expected to do the opposite of these things. If such aims as maintaining economic stability and controlling inflation are intended to serve the national interest, then if the means to these ends by witting or unwitting design involves impoverishing some members of the nation or excluding them from opportunities to participate in the benefits sought for, the principle that all in a democracy have an equal claim on the state's concern and respect is violated.

This point can be made clearer by adapting Rawls' idea of an 'original position', as already hinted above. It involves asking what kind of socio-political arrangements people would choose to accept if, behind a 'veil of ignorance', not knowing what their position or circumstances in society would be, they could do so. They do not know what social class they will be born into, how intelligent, talented, or healthy they will be, what values, beliefs, and ambitions they might come to have, nor even what kind of society it is. They will only know that 'circumstances of justice', as Rawls calls them, will apply, and that the situation will be one of moderate scarcity of resources, which means that the moral and political views of the society's members will determine the distribution of those resources.

Rawls argues that people behind the veil of ignorance would apply what is known as a 'maximin' strategy for choosing the nature of the society. This is a strategy in game theory that makes the *most* of the *least* that can be reliably anticipated in a given situation. On this basis, Rawls says, people would choose to apply the following two principles of justice: first, that each member of society should have an equal right to the greatest degree of basic liberty compatible with everyone else's basic liberty, and second, that inequalities in society should be so arranged that they provide the greatest benefit possible to the least advantaged, and should not prevent offices and positions from being open to everyone under conditions of 'fair equality of opportunity'.

Rawls' governing idea is that justice is *fairness*, and on that basis he postulates a society so arranged that it ensures a distribution of social goods and burdens to which reflective citizens will consent and in which they will cooperate. He assumes that arbitrary advantages – being born with talent or into a rich family – do not merit a larger share of the distribution; the distribution has to be equal unless everyone would benefit from an unequal distribution.

Because the 'veil of ignorance' exists to mask the occupants of the original position from knowing what their own circumstances will be on entering the society, it therefore trades on a conception of 'enlightened self-interest' in which each individual will choose to protect himself as much as possible from the disadvantages of being at the worst-off level. But let us adjust the Rawlsian view somewhat. Suppose that instead of prompting us to choose an arrangement that protects us lest we find ourselves at the bottom of the heap, it makes us rational and disinterested in our view of what follows from being democrats, that is, holders of the view that each member of society has an equal right to participate in the life of the society and in the choice of the laws and government under which it will operate, and to be treated with the state's and the society's concern and respect equally with everyone else. What would we think are the reasonable expectations that we and fellow citizens would be entitled to have?

Consider these suggestions: that it would be reasonable to expect that there should not be avoidable barriers to participation in society's opportunities. Such barriers include lack of education, treatable illness, lack of information about what is happening and what opportunities are available in society, deliberate exclusion from those opportunities on the grounds of race, ethnicity, sex, sexuality, age, and religion, inequality before the law, and economic policies designed to favour only part of the population. The further suggestion is that the concept of democracy itself entails that the state *should* ensure as a matter of positive public policy that such barriers do not exist.

This can be summarized as saying that the concept of *democracy* – embodying the principles of *participation and equal concern* – entails that social justice is a mandatory aim. This can scarcely be a surprise. Yet the view that government's purpose does not extend beyond the less ambitious one of protection of liberty and property, and that further amenities of life are to be secured by private endeavour only – even if this means that resultant inequalities can grow so large as to exclude sections of society from access to them – is inconsistent with it.

Collecting the considerations discussed in the foregoing, we might suggest that the purpose of government in a democratic order is as follows. Government exists to establish justice, ensure domestic tranquillity, provide for common defence, protect and promote civil liberties, overcome barriers to participation in the civil, political, and economic life of the state in order to promote social justice, and enhance or at least encourage the development of culture. The *manner* in which democratic government pursues these aims is by treating all citizens with equal concern and respect. This is less anodyne than it appears. For one striking point about putting matters like this is that it implies that the purpose of *government* in a democracy is to transcend factionalism of all kinds in pursuit of a common commitment to the idea that aspirations towards good lives in a good society matter. *Party* politics, which in its essence is factional, exists to serve one or more of a special set of interests – the interests of a class (whether upper, middle, or working class), a money interest, a religious interest, a business interest, a workers' interest. Serving an interest is legitimate, and political activity in which the interests are urged and debated is not merely important but essential to democracy, where all ideas and desires require to be aired and to test themselves against one another. But *government* cannot be annexed to a single such interest if it is to be *government in a democracy*, that is, the government of all the people, among whom all these interests have their place. Accordingly, government has to find a way of respecting the competition of interests and aspirations but simultaneously of acting according to the best overall interest. This too is a political matter, but this time it is the politics not of faction but of compromise and agreement. It is a key point that the government that emerges from politics is government *for the people* and not *by a faction of the people in its own interests*. When it is the latter – as it standardly is in our contemporary democracies – it is *not fulfilling the purposes of democratic government.*

Again to adapt a familiar catchphrase: democratic government is instituted and authorized *by the people* to act *for the people*; it is not instituted so that some of the people can capture government in order to act in the interests of some of the people. This point iterates, from a different direction, the idea that government should in a significant sense be above politics. Politics and government should be kept apart as much as possible. Politics belongs in election campaigns, in the act of voting, in the negotiations between those elected to form a government – for in an electoral system that reflects the diversity of preferences in society, negotiation to form a coalition government can be expected to be standard practice. Then, once the politics has been dealt with, the business of government, for all the people, can be got on with. Why should this idea be surprising as an implication of democracy, whose fundamental idea is that the enfranchised come together to empower a government to manage affairs in a way that will optimize matters for *all* the state's citizens? Government *by politics* is government by the party or faction that 'won' and keeps out the others so that it can implement its side of the political divide. What we see in the UK and US is this: the FPTP electoral system keeps a two-party arrangement in existence with the enfranchised being offered a Hobson's Choice over the take-it-all-or-leave-it manifestos offered by the two parties. This is very far from an optimal democracy, and in reality it does not produce government *for the people* but instead only *for those who voted for the winners.* The concept of democracy, in a pluralistic society in which there are ranges of interests and needs, is not the concept of a system in which government is captured by whichever side of a disagreement 'wins', but instead is the concept of governing by agreement; of reaching a shared view among all the representatives of the people on a programme they can work together to deliver in the interests of all.

Democracy implies government by coalition; it implies reducing the political content of the operation of government; it implies as a principle the idea that government transcends party politics.

3

POWERS AND INSTITUTIONS

The undemocratic nature of the FPTP voting system used in the US, the UK, and a number of other Westminster-derived systems, speaks for itself – and so loudly that a number of Westminster-derived systems have addressed and sought to remedy the problem by introducing electoral systems that are more proportionate, though not always satisfactorily so, for example Australia and New Zealand. If this were the only major difficulty with the model, there would be less urgency for further reform. But in fact it is not even the greatest problem with the Westminster Model. The greatest problem is the model's failure to institutionalize a *separation of powers* among the principal organs of state. The effect is to subvert the intrinsic point of what democracy, by its very definition, is intended to be.

When the Founders of the United States were considering how to structure the institutions of the federal government, one of their main sources of inspiration was the writings of Montesquieu – Charles-Louis de Secondat, baron de Montesquieu – in his book *De l'esprit des lois* (1748), literally *The Spirit of Laws* but most often called in English *The Spirit of the Laws*. One of Montesquieu's principal arguments concerned the structure of government, and in particular the way that the structure could insure against abuses of power – a concern for all who had witnessed absolute monarchy either at first hand (as Montesquieu himself had done in the France of Louis XIV, who died in 1715 when Montesquieu was a young man) or in the recent past of the countries they lived in; or who had meditated on the implications of Hobbes' 'Leviathan', the absolute sovereign power against whom or which the only possible appeal, and this in the sole case of failure to protect the people's lives, was revolution. Montesquieu wrote, 'All would be lost if the same man, or the same body of leaders – whether from among the nobles or from among the people – were to exercise these three powers: that of making laws, that of executing public resolutions, and that of judging crimes or disputes between individuals.'[1] This in effect states a principle: the principle of the separation of powers.

Montesquieu expanded the point thus:

> When the legislative and executive powers are united in the same person, or in the same body of magistrates, there can be no liberty . . . Again, there is no liberty, if the judicial power be not separated from the legislative and executive. Were it joined with the legislative, the life and liberty of the subject would be exposed to arbitrary control; for the judge would then be the legislator. Were it joined to the executive power, the judge might behave with violence and oppression. There would be an end to everything, were the same man, or the same body, whether of the nobles or the people, to exercise those three powers.[2]

Montesquieu took eighteenth-century England as his model of a state in which – as he thought – a separation of powers existed, adding to his own observations, made while living there, the writings of Locke following the constitutional settlement of the 'Glorious Revolution' of 1688. Locke's explanation for approving of the point that 'in all moderated Monarchies and well-framed Governments [the] Legislative and Executive Power are in distinct hands', is that:

> it may be too great a temptation to human frailty apt to grasp at Power, for the same Persons who have the Power of making Laws, to have also in their hands the power to execute them, whereby they may exempt themselves from Obedience to the Laws they make, and suit the Law, both in its making and execution, to their own private advantage, and thereby come to have a distinct interest from the rest of the Community, contrary to the end of Society and Government.[3]

In citing the example of the English constitution, Montesquieu was using it as an indicative model rather than a template. He saw the two houses of the legislature – the House of Commons and the House of Lords – as carrying out the legislative function, the Crown as the executive, and the judiciary as independent of both. This is not in fact how matters lay with the English arrangements, in which powers were not separated by institution, but distributed within the same institution: Parliament. This is because Parliament is technically composed of Crown, Lords, and Commons together, and therefore the executive arm – the Crown and the ministers appointed by the Crown from among Members of Parliament (at that time the most senior ministerial appointments often came from the House of Lords) – and the legislative arm were indistinct.

Moreover Locke had not treated the judiciary as one of three separate *loci* of power, but instead nominated what he called the 'federative' power as separate from the legislative and executive powers, this being the power to make war and peace and enter into treaties with foreign governments.[4] In Locke, therefore, the concept of the separation of powers was not the same as the separation of institutions, one each for each of the powers. Instead the idea was one of *distribution* of powers *within* the institution of Parliament: the legislative and executive arms of government were institutionally indistinct, though exercising distinguishable offices.

But this was not an excuse for maintaining a situation which allows a yielding to the 'too great temptation' to have the power of making and applying law in the same hands. In the *Seven Bishops* case of 1688 one of the presiding justices remarked that if a power to suspend laws were left in the King's hands 'there will need no parliament: all the legislature will be in the King' – a remark that would have resonated powerfully in that courtroom as a reference to the great struggle between Charles I and Parliament which had precipitated the Civil War.[5] The problematic question of prerogative powers remains; though in practice the powers are now exercisable only by the government of the day, the fact that their use bypasses Parliament is a crux. For Locke the question of the separation of *powers* between the Lords' and Commons' legislative control of the Crown's actions, and the Crown's executive power independently of the two Houses of Parliament, was therefore not just a live issue but the pressing issue of the moment, which the new post-1688 settlement expressly addressed – and resolved to the benefit of Parliament. (Judicial independence in England was only fully secured at last in the Act of Settlement 1701.)

It would have been natural enough for the newly independent Americans to develop a model for their institutions from arrangements they were familiar with. The parallels between the two Houses of Congress and Britain's two Houses of Parliament,

and between King and President though with the highly significant difference of the latter's functional as well as institutional
separation from Congress, are obvious. A judiciary independent
of both is a modification of the original in constitutional terms,
not in practice; the fact of the English judiciary's independence
as established at the beginning of the eighteenth century was
doubtless a motive for later reference to it as the third element in
the array of powers. A key reason for annexing the separation of
powers to a separation of institutions is however apparent in
Montesquieu's view that one of the great benefits of such a separation is that it provides *checks and balances* within government,
each of the powers acting as a counterweight to the others. This,
as constitution-making proceeded in America at the end of the
eighteenth century, was a prompt for the American colonists in
the design of their new institutions.

It is moot whether Montesquieu intended the principle of the
separation of powers to be realized in an actual separation of institutions. It has been persuasively argued that his 'concern is not
that the three powers must each be in separate pairs of hands but
that no two of them should be placed in a single pair of hands. He
achieves this, and thinks that England achieves it, by placing both
of two powers in three pairs of hands. It is a solution to the problem of the tendency of power to corrupt.'[6] This sees Montesquieu
as adopting the same position as Locke; and this point of view
also includes Locke's exclusion of the judiciary from the position
of third locus in Montesquieu's taxonomy of institutions.

The reading of Montesquieu given by some of the Founders
in America was different from this. It prompted them to the
view that a separation of powers is best effected by a separation
of institutions. In the Constitution of Massachusetts (1780),
written by John Adams, Article XXX says:

In the government of this commonwealth, the legislative department shall never exercise the executive and judicial powers, or
either of them: the executive shall never exercise the legislative
and judicial powers, or either of them: the judicial shall never
exercise the legislative and executive powers, or either of them:
to the end it may be a government of laws and not of men.

In *Federalist Papers* No. 47, Madison begins by asserting, or
appearing to assert, a similar view: 'The accumulation of all
powers, legislative, executive and judiciary, in the same hands,
whether of one, a few, or many, and whether hereditary, self-
appointed, or elective, may justly be pronounced the very definition of tyranny.'[7]

But Madison then temporizes, on the basis that Montesquieu
had taken his cue from the British constitution and that this
latter was one in which the powers were distributed not
separated:

he did not mean that these departments [the legislative, executive, and judicial] ought to have *no partial agency* in, or no *control*
over, the acts of each other. His meaning [is] that where the
whole power of one department is exercised by the same hands
which possess the *whole* power of another department, the
fundamental principles of a free constitution are subverted.

Madison is attempting to solve the practical problem that
whereas a separation of powers is constitutionally essential, it is
difficult to achieve in practice institutionally. Arguably, therefore, his argument here is a sleight of hand. A 'partial agency in'
a power is not the same thing as 'control over' the exercise of a
power by another agency, as in, say, a judicial review finding that
a law passed by a legislature is unconstitutional. This would be

to exert a measure of control, without having had any agency in framing and passing the law in the first place.

In fact one can see the problem clearly outlined in Madison's own immediately following words: 'the fundamental principles of a free constitution are subverted [if] the King, who is the sole executive magistrate, had possessed also the complete legislative power, or the supreme administration of justice; or if the entire legislative body had possessed the supreme judiciary, or the supreme executive authority.' *For this is exactly the situation in which Westminster Model democracies* (other than the US version and certain derivative hybrids) *stand*: the executive is drawn from the majority in the legislature, and therefore both controls it and is indistinguishable from it; and where, as in the case of the UK, there is no constitutional check on the power of the legislature (and hence no check on the executive which controls the legislature) there is as absolute a power in the executive's hands as there was in that of any absolute monarch in history.

In terms more similar to Adams' than to Madison's view, the National Conference of State Legislatures (NCSL) in today's US states in its publications that Montesquieu's writings:

> inspired the Declaration of the Rights of Man and the Constitution of the United States. Under his model, the political authority of the state is divided into legislative, executive and judicial powers. He asserted that, to promote liberty most effectively, these three powers must be separate and acting independently.
>
> Separation of powers, therefore, refers to the division of government responsibilities into distinct branches to limit any one branch from exercising the core functions of another. The intent is to prevent the concentration of power and provide for checks and balances.

The traditional characterizations of the powers of the branches of American government are:

- The legislative branch is responsible for enacting the laws of the state and appropriating the money necessary to operate the government.
- The executive branch is responsible for implementing and administering the public policy enacted and funded by the legislative branch.
- The judicial branch is responsible for interpreting the constitution and laws and applying their interpretations to controversies brought before it.

Forty state constitutions specify that government be divided into three branches: legislative, executive and judicial. California illustrates this approach; "The powers of state government are legislative, executive, and judicial. Persons charged with the exercise of one power may not exercise either of the others except as permitted by this Constitution."[8]

The NCSL webpage then adds a rider: 'While separation of powers is key to the workings of American government, no democratic system exists with an absolute separation of powers ... Governmental powers and responsibilities ... are too complex and interrelated to be neatly compartmentalized.' This remark expresses a pragmatic view which appears hard to gainsay. But an apparently similar view shows that at the fundamental level of the powers of government, the separation is as *de facto* sharp as it is *de jure* clear, demonstrated by such provisions in the US as the bar on members of the legislative branch serving in the executive branch and vice versa.

The apparently similar view in question owes itself to Sir Ivor Jennings, one of the small number of authorities most often cited on the British constitution. He wrote: 'The existence of an elected legislature necessarily implies a separation of powers, not because it is possible to distinguish functions of government into three classes, but simply because an assembly is not a suitable body to control detailed administration or to decide whether the laws have been broken or not.'[9] One immediately notes that Jennings' understanding of the exercise of government's functions implies not only a *'distribution* rather than a *separation'* model, but one based on merely utilitarian grounds rather than principle. In the Westminster Model such distribution indeed happens, and for this selfsame utilitarian reason; but *effective* power lies in just one of the institutions – the executive – through its control of the legislature; and therefore the distribution is in fact a delegation merely, and a revocable one.

Suppose a defence of the Westminster Model's lack of a constitutional separation of powers is offered on the pragmatic ground that a *de facto* distribution of powers is good enough by itself. Given that the intention of a separation of powers is to bring the activities of government into a system of checks and balances, it can be argued that this is achieved in practice by a distribution alone. So, if some executive powers lie with a legislature and some legislative powers with the associated executive, either or both these circumstances can obtain: that the legislature's executive powers have domains of application different from those of the executive; or, mechanisms can exist which resolve a conflict of exercise of powers, for example by recognizing the superior authority of the legislature, as the popularly elected body, over the executive however constituted.

This defence might further cite the fact that in any case the distribution is *merely* pragmatic, and a 'last resort' appeal to *de jure* separation is always available. In the US the question does not arise because the executive (the President) is elected independently of Congress. But in the UK the executive holds some 'prerogative powers', including law-making ones, independently of Parliament, and in all Common Law jurisdictions the practice of 'judge-made law' continues, even if inferior to statute; so here the *de jure* last resort exists.

This defence does not, however, persuade. It does not remove or mitigate the fact that in all (non-US) Westminster Model polities *the executive controls the legislature,* and that therefore the checks that separation is intended to ensure are wholly absent – except in the unusual and usually temporary circumstances of minority government.[10] In the US version there is a different but no less serious failure: the *absence of a boundary between the political processes of the legislative and executive branches and the upper reaches of the judiciary*: Supreme Court and Appeals Court justices are appointed jointly by the legislative and executive branches – *and on party-political terms.*

In the UK and many of the parliamentary systems derived from it, the executive – the government: the Prime Minister and cabinet members – is drawn from the majority in the House of Commons. Because of the system of party discipline exercised through the whips who ensure that the government's majority delivers its programme, the effect is that the legislature is the creature of the executive, not its master; the legislature is under the executive's control, not holding the executive to account but, instead, carrying out its behests.[11] It is only in circumstances where the executive no longer controls a majority in the House of Commons that the legislature can begin to control it in turn. Even this is not as straightforward as it might seem, because a sitting government has great influence over the procedures and legislative timetable of the House of Commons, and can use this to resist the efforts of the legislature to hold it to account. A classic instance of just such circumstances is afforded by the UK

House of Commons in 2018–19 during the minority administration of the Conservative Party when it was attempting to deal
with the Brexit debacle caused by the 2016 EU referendum.

The history of the executive takeover of the legislature in the
House of Commons is the history of an accident: the inability of
George I of Great Britain to speak English. Since the accession
of William III in 1688 it had come to be accepted that the 'cabinet' of the King – the small inner circle of counsellors holding
high offices of state – was a legitimate organ of administration,
though until that time the existence of such a thing had been
regarded with suspicion as a cabal within the larger Privy
Council that had for centuries been the body of advisors to the
Crown.[12] When the Duke of Hanover succeeded to the British
throne as King George I on the death of Queen Anne in 1714,
the recently formed but effective administrative arrangement of
the 'cabinet' was well-placed to manage national affairs without
the close intervention of a king who, unable to follow the discussions or read the state papers without the aid of translation, from
1717 onwards ceased to attend cabinet meetings and relied
instead on periodic consultations about its activities and decisions. In the decades that followed, especially after the South
Sea Bubble affair of 1721, the powerful personality of Sir Robert
Walpole increasingly came to define the role of 'Prime Minister'
– though this label was at first a pejorative, and was only formally
and officially recognized as late as 1878 when Benjamin Disraeli
employed it in signing the Treaty of Berlin of that year. In 1885
Hansard, the record of parliamentary debates, began to use the
title 'Prime Minister' formally.

However, *The Times* had used the description 'Prime
Minister' as early as 1805, and the reality of the office was well
understood and entrenched much earlier, and certainly by the
time of Lord North – the politician who lost the North

American colonies in the 1770s. The point of interest for present purposes is that in the cabinets of monarchs before 1688 – the private sub-committees of the Privy Council – and in the more openly accepted cabinets of William III and Queen Anne, the members were chiefly peers and therefore, coincidentally, members of the House of Lords. But it was only by this coincidence that they were parliamentarians. The Crown could have appointed a non-parliamentarian to ministerial position if it chose, though in effect it had long been the case either that peers, as members of the court, would receive such office, or that commoners appointed to such office would be elevated to the peerage.

After 1688 Parliament's control of the money supply increased its power greatly *vis à vis* the Crown, and therefore membership of Parliament by members of the cabinet came to matter. As the power and influence of the House of Commons grew in the nineteenth century commensurately with the extension of the franchise, most especially after the mid-nineteenth century when it became increasingly uncommon and eventually – as a pragmatic matter – impossible for a member of the House of Lords to serve as Prime Minister, the power of the cabinet and its control of the House of Commons was complete.[13] Indeed within the cabinet the power of the Prime Minister had grown great: William Gladstone wrote in 1878 that 'nowhere in the wide world does so great a substance cast so small a shadow; nowhere is there a man who has so much power, with so little to show for it in the way of formal title or prerogative'.[14]

In the UK (until 1801 the country was known as Great Britain) the story of the growth of cabinet government is the story of the growth of executive control of the legislature. In the US – to repeat – the failure of separation exists not between executive and legislature but between the political processes both in Congress and the White House, on the one hand, and the upper reaches of the judiciary on the other hand.

Appointments to the bench of the Supreme Court, and to vacant seats in the Courts of Appeal, are made by the President subject to confirmation by the Senate. Both these aspects of judicial appointments are therefore infected by party-political considerations. A classic example is the controversial appointment of Justice Brett Kavanaugh to the Supreme Court in 2018, and the delay imposed by a Republican-dominated Senate in confirming numerous federal judges in the closing years of President Obama's second term. Many other examples of the politics of judicial appointments can be cited over the course of American history. Appeals Court and Supreme Court justices serve for life, and both have enormous influence over the interpretation and application of the law and the Constitution in the US. The power of Appeals Court justices is evidenced by the fact that in the twelve circuits (eleven regional plus the Federal Circuit) nearly 8000 cases are decided annually, fewer than 2% of which are reviewed by the Supreme Court. This implies an extensive influence over American life and society, so the political complexion of appointments matters. The fact that appointments have a political complexion at all is the point at issue, revealing the complete failure of a crucial separation between the institutions of governance.

Throughout this discussion so far a significant point has been left in abeyance. This is that no writers on this matter appear to recognize a vital distinction between *powers* and *functions*. An organ of government might have certain functions – the implementation of policy, say – but not the correlative powers – in this case, the making of policy. Consider a polity in which the legislature and executive occupy separate institutions, but both are able to propose legislation although only the legislature can

71

vote the proposals into law. They share a function – proposing legislation – but not a power – voting the legislation into law. The judiciary, in pronouncing on the constitutionality of laws, or in 'making law' by modifying precedent or establishing precedent in interpretations of statute, partially share a function and a power with the legislature, though its power in this regard is subordinate to that of the legislature, which can make laws that override judicial interpretations of existing laws. And the judiciary shares a power with the executive in enforcing the law (imposing penalties, finding defaulters in contempt, and the like) though lacking the executive's function of making enforcement effective through its instruments (such as the police).[15]

For historical reasons the distinction between powers and functions has come to be blurred, and the possession of a function has suggested to the dull eye[16] that it is always – instead of only sometimes – tantamount to a power, and vice versa. In the English Parliament of 1688 the Houses of Commons and Lords acquired some of the Crown's powers to add to the functions they performed; in the reigns of the early Hanoverians the cabinet of ministers acquired both further powers and functions, blended; with the extension of the franchise in the nineteenth and twentieth centuries, entailing an increasing need for party discipline and control,[17] the blended power and function of the executive became absolute whenever the party of government had a majority over all others in the elected House, which has usually been the case.

The obvious solution to the separation-of-powers problem is to introduce arrangements in which the legislative, executive, and judicial powers are exercised by different institutions, distinguished by function; that the executive power is answerable to the legislative power, that the judicial power is controlled by neither of the other powers, that both are reviewable by the judicial power as to the constitutionality and legality of their actions, but that the judicial power is not a permanent obstacle to the legislative power.

The objection urged against institutional separation of powers by upholders of the Westminster Model is that it is a great advantage to have government ministers drawn from among the members of the legislature, because they are immediately accountable to it as sitting among the legislators and scrutinizable by them there. This is described as 'responsible government' by defenders of the system; the executors are immediately responsible to the legislators sitting around them in the Parliament house. The practices of Prime Minister's Questions every week in the UK House of Commons, together with questions to ministers both in the body of the legislature and by Select Committees drawn from the legislature, are replicated in similar forms in other Westminster Model legislatures, and are standardly cited as examples.[18]

This objection is, however, very readily answered. An executive's being separate from the legislature does not stop the members of the executive being regularly questioned by the legislature in exactly the same way as at present in the Westminster Model, both on the floor of the legislative house before all members, and by committees appointed for the task. The latter is the case in Congress in the US; the minor novelty suggested in addition here is that members of the executive should regularly be present in the body of the legislature to present their proposals, explain and defend them, take questions, and listen to suggestions and objections, as happens in France – thus reprising the current situation, but with the important difference that members of the executive do not vote on proposals as well as carrying them out, thus participating in endorsing the laws they are charged with applying.

If a Westminster Model system does not reform itself so that the executive no longer controls the legislature, but as now remains in command of it, the second-best arrangement is one in which a proportional system of representation results in a lower likelihood that a single party will dominate the legislature. Coalition governments will temper the dangers inherent in the 'elective tyranny' (as a British Lord Chancellor, Lord Hailsham, described it)[19] that the Westminster Model consists in. Hailsham, although a Conservative politician, had concluded that the system was unsafe: governments which control the legislature have unlimited powers to do what they like, and the fact of a Westminster Model Parliament's absolute sovereignty was dramatized by Sir Leslie Stephen's remark, made as long ago as 1882, that if Parliament 'decided that all blue-eyed babies should be murdered, the preservation of blue-eyed babies would be illegal'.[20] This is as true today as it was when he wrote it. Codification of the constitutional arrangements describing the powers, and their limits, of the executive are therefore a necessity in all cases: it is remarkable that in some of the advanced states of the twenty-first century there should be systems of government whose powers are unspecified, leaving the 'blue-eyed babies' problem to be controlled by the 'gentlemanly proclivities' of politicians respecting 'conventions'. That is how things are in the UK, Canada and other places today. To remedy this, there has to be separation of powers, or at very least systems of representation which are genuinely proportional and thus entail that government will standardly be multi-party in composition.

These considerations relate directly to the fulfilment of what is entailed by the concept of democracy: that the policies of government must be in the interests of all, and their implementation transparent and accountable to all. Keeping the three powers of state separate is a chief means to these ends.

And here the final point bites: a separation of powers does not imply an equality of powers. The legislature, consisting of the directly elected representatives, must hold the superior power in making law, though the law – while in operation – remains superior to all. The judicial power is tasked with ensuring compliance with, and proper interpretation of, the law, while the legislature keeps that law in being. The executive is tasked with applying the laws and administering the agencies carrying out the objectives of the laws. And because the legislators serve at the pleasure of the enfranchised, the result is that a democracy is a realm of rule by law – recall Livy: 'the rule of law, not of men' – and the functions of office (not of the office-holders) are matters ultimately controlled by the enfranchised, on whose behalf the members of the legislature and the other organs of governance serve while they have the enfranchised's permission.

4

POLITICS AND PEOPLE

The quality of people in a democracy determines the quality of the democracy. One can ask what the enfranchised in a democracy would ideally be like, why such ideals are never attained, and what to do about it: can the causes of that non-ideality be addressed, or must a democracy cater for the effects of that non-ideality?

One can consider the people of a democracy under four headings: voters, political activists, politicians, and journalists. Among the questions to be asked about each group are the following. Regarding voters, the questions are: 'What would an ideal voter in a democracy be like? Given that no democracy is ever likely to have ideal voters, what can be done to enhance the democratic value of voters and voter participation?'

Regarding activists and politicians, the questions are: 'What would we wish our politicians to be like, and – again given the impossibility of perfection – what can be done to keep politicians to the highest standards of service and probity? What is the role and extent of influence of political activists in party affairs and candidate selection? What constraints should there be on the appointment of non-Civil Service unelected paid advisors to politicians and ministers?'

Regarding journalists – I use the term to embrace all who engage in opinion and debate in all media including social media – the questions are: 'What would we wish the sources of information and debate to be like in the public domain? Given the impossibility that there will be, on all media platforms, universal truthfulness, sober judgment, careful analysis, and responsible debate, what can be done to ensure that voters get accurate and reliable information upon which to base their voting decisions?'

These questions are about what, from the human side of the matter, can make the institutional arrangements and practices of a polity function so that it both accords with the principles of democracy and satisfies the purposes of government. Obviously, a political order with a careless and uninterested populace, unprincipled politicians, hijacking of the constitutional process by small groups of vigorous and tendentiously motivated activists and 'advisors', and communications media driven by such extreme partisanship and individual polemical imperative that it freely and frequently deploys falsehood, is in danger of creating, sooner or later, a dysfunctional state.[1] The questions to be asked about the players in the political order are therefore questions about how to avoid this.

To set the scene for discussion of one aspect of these questions, consider what the Harvard University political scientists Steven Levitsky and Daniel Ziblatt say in their book *How Democracies Die* (2018) about how the US political system until recently maintained 'gatekeepers' against threats to American democracy. Their argument is that two 'unwritten democratic norms' governing politicians' behaviour sustained the functioning of the constitution 'in ways that we have come to take for granted: mutual toleration, or the understanding that competing parties accept one another as legitimate rivals, and forbearance, or the idea that politicians should exercise restraint in deploying their institutional prerogatives'.[2]

They are here in effect channelling John Stuart Mill, who introduced the idea – previously mentioned – of 'constitutional morality' as what, in optimal circumstances, individuals will observe so that they act with restraint and judiciousness either when electing representatives or serving in Parliament and government. Mill wrote:

> In imperfectly balanced governments, where some attempt is made to set constitutional limits to the impulses of the strongest power, but where that power is strong enough to overstep them with at least temporary impunity, it is only by doctrines of constitutional morality, recognized and sustained by opinion, that any regard at all is preserved for the checks and limitations of the constitution. In well-balanced governments, in which the supreme power is divided, and each sharer is protected against the usurpations of the others in the only manner possible – namely, by being armed for defence with weapons as strong as the others can wield for attack – the government can only be carried on by forbearance on all sides to exercise those extreme powers, unless provoked by conduct equally extreme on the part of some other sharer of power: and in this case we may truly say that only by the regard paid to maxims of constitutional morality is the constitution kept in existence.[3]

The question immediately to be asked is whether this hope – that individual politicians and parties will act with restraint and forbearance, not using the powers they have to the fullest extent in order to preserve the constitution on the gentlemanly basis of an informal or unwritten sense of 'constitutional morality' – is a realistic one. Levitsky and Ziblatt claim that it is a realistic hope, on the grounds that this in fact is what, until recently (that is, until the Trump era), kept the American Constitution in balance. They cite as examples the way that such disruptive and populist American political figures as Father Charles Coughlin, Huey Long, Joseph McCarthy, and George Wallace were resisted by the internal workings of political party organizations.[4]

This claim is questionable. In the case of the popular and radical radio priest Father Charles Coughlin, pressure was brought on the Catholic Church to restrain him, and various bureaucratic moves were made by the incumbent President Franklin D. Roosevelt to censor him, by denying him a broadcast licence and Post Office facilities for distribution of his magazine. In the case of Huey Long and George Wallace, it was the assassin's bullet that brought their careers to an end – Long was shot to death in September 1935, and Wallace was shot and paralysed in May 1972 during his third attempt at securing the Democratic Party nomination to run for the Presidency. Wheelchair-bound, he tried again in 1976 as an independent, but voter perceptions of his health status and disability stood in the way. While hospitalized in 1972 Wallace was visited not only by party allies but by political opponents also; among the visitors were Richard Nixon, Spiro Agnew, and Ted Kennedy, and among senders of goodwill telegrams were Ronald Reagan and the Pope. As a four-time governor of Alabama and a four-time presidential hopeful Wallace can hardly be viewed as someone prevented by any party-political machine from having a highly visible and influential career, even if he did not make it through the presidential primaries – because, in the end, of a would-be assassin's bullet.

Moreover John F. Kennedy, Martin Luther King, and Robert Kennedy had assassins' bullets rather than political opposition to blame for the curtailment of their endeavours, unless of course the murders themselves are to be counted as a method of political opposition. Whether or not the assassins in question were deranged soloists or agents of political conspiracies, either way they do not constitute the kind of self-restraint implied by 'unwritten norms' or 'constitutional morality' in the sense intended by Levitsky, Ziblatt, and Mill.

A formal, institutional gatekeeper in the constitutional arrangements of the US is the Electoral College, designed to ensure the fitness of candidates for the country's highest office. The Electoral College is intended, as the US Constitution's Article II states, to consist of 'men most capable of analysing the qualities adapted to the station, and acting under circumstances favourable to deliberation, and to a judicious combination of all the reasons and inducements which were proper to govern them'. The Electors would be the ones actually to appoint the President, thus ensuring in Alexander Hamilton's words that 'the office of President will seldom fall to the lot of any man who is not in an eminent degree endowed with the requisite qualifications'. Whatever the merits of the idea, its objective was almost immediately negated by the seizure of the process by party politics at the beginning of the nineteenth century. The Founders had imagined a group of notables of Olympian detachment having the final say on who was fit to serve in the White House, but as soon as rival political parties became the nominators of who was to serve on the Electoral College, its purpose was vitiated.[5]

Levitsky and Ziblatt say that the Founders had not anticipated this; they 'did not seriously contemplate those parties' existence'.[6] On the contrary, it would seem clear from *Federalist Papers* No. 10 that James Madison was acutely aware of the danger of 'faction' – of which party-political division is the prime example – even though he later went on to be a founder of the Democratic Party, thus in effect belying his own strictures.[7] He described faction as a 'dangerous vice' because of the 'instability, injustice and confusion' that it introduces into the 'public counsels'. Everywhere, he said, he heard complaints from 'our most considerate and virtuous citizens . . . that the public good is disregarded in the conflicts of rival parties'. This sounds, alas, all too familiar.

Madison said that the cure for faction was either to remove the cause of it, or to control its effects. Removing the cause of it would involve either 'destroying the liberty which is essential to its existence', or 'giving to every citizen the same opinions, the same passions, and the same interests'. Obviously, the first is undesirable and the second impracticable. To destroy liberty is worse than accepting that faction must arise from it. Liberty is to faction what air is to fire; but to annihilate air in order to put out fire would kill us all.

Equally obvious is the impracticability of making everyone think and feel the same: 'As long as the reason of man continues fallible, and he is at liberty to exercise it, different opinions will be formed . . . The latent causes of faction are thus sown in the nature of man'. Differences over religion, over who should hold the government, over public policy on matters of the economy and society, and above all differences arising from disparities in property and wealth, generate competition, friction, and mutual animosities, eventually even over 'the most frivolous and fanciful distinctions'.[8]

Nor, says Madison, can we hope that some enlightened statesman will appear who will 'adjust these clashing interests and render them all subservient to the public good. Enlightened helmsmen will not always be at the helm' – thus reprising the lesson of Han Fei's farmer and hare.

The answer must therefore be the second option mentioned: controlling the *effects* of faction. When the disruption is caused by a faction in the minority, it can be dealt with by majority opposition. Matters are more problematic when the faction holds the majority in relevant organs of government. 'To secure the public good and private rights against the danger of such a faction, and at the same time to preserve the spirit and the form of popular government, is then the great object to which our enquiries are directed.' Madison adds that achieving this aim is the only way that democracy as a form of political order can be rescued from the bad light in which it had stood since Plato: this aim 'is the great desideratum by which alone this form of government can be rescued from the opprobrium under which it has so long laboured, and be recommended to the esteem and adoption of mankind'.[9]

So how is it to be done? There are only two options, Madison says. Either a factional majority – one that seeks to act in ways that involve the positive detriment of those outside it – must be prevented from forming in the first place, or it must be rendered incapable of carrying its schemes into effect. In small democracies such as Greek city states it is nigh impossible to prevent a simple majority from oppressing a minority or an individual, but in a democracy of the kind being set up in North America at the time that Madison was writing, there is a remedy: *representation* – the delegation of government to a body of chosen citizens 'whose wisdom may best discern the true interest of their country and whose patriotism and love of justice will be least likely to sacrifice it to temporary or partial considerations'. In such circumstances 'the public voice, pronounced by the representatives of the people, will be more consonant to the public good than if pronounced by the people themselves'. Of course, 'men of factious tempers, of local prejudices, or of sinister designs' might capture the suffrage of the people by 'intrigue, corruption, or other means', and then 'betray the interests of the people'. This is more likely to happen in small societies. But in a large and populous society this is less likely to happen, Madison argued, because 'men of factious tempers' are less likely to be able to suborn a large number of voters than a small number.[10]

This last point – that a large democracy is safer from faction than a small one – was intended by Madison to support his case for a federal union of the states that had become independent of Great Britain, rather than leaving them merely as a loose confederation or alliance of independent states. That was the overall aim of the *Federalist Papers*, after all, as their very name suggests. The history of democracy both in America and elsewhere has, however, demonstrated that even large democracies are not immune to faction and its distorting effects – even with the form of representative democracy Madison extols. And this immunity has all but vanished in the age of social media, through which the long-standing political practices of propaganda, spin, half-truths, untruths, and false promises have been weaponized.[11] But the whole of Madison's argument is exceedingly interesting from the point of view of what it says and implies about the theme of this chapter – the question of *the people of a democracy*.

For one thing, he is right that the inevitability of faction – of the partisanship, divisions, and conflicts of party politics – can only be fully met by 'controlling its effects' rather than trying to prevent its causes. Of course there has to be an endeavour to get voters and those they vote for to work for the public good rather than merely factional interests, but given that it is no good *relying* on success in this, the question has to be: 'What *institutions and rules of practice* can be arranged to mitigate the *effects* of faction to prevent it militating against the public good?' This key question is addressed in chapter 6. The idea is also well articulated by Madison when he considers, in *Federalist Papers* No. 51, the reason why formal constraints have to be imposed on politicians and government ministers:

> Ambition must be made to counteract ambition. The interest of the man must be connected with the constitutional rights of the place. It may be a reflection on human nature, that such devices should be necessary to controul the abuses of government. But what is government itself but the greatest of all reflections on human nature? If men were angels, no government would be necessary. If angels were to govern men, neither external nor internal controuls on government would be necessary. In framing a government which is to be administered by men over men, the great difficulty lies in this: You must first enable the government to controul the governed; and in the next place, oblige it to controul itself. A dependence on the people is no doubt the primary controul on the government; but experience has taught mankind the necessity of auxiliary precautions.[12]

But there is still something to be said about dealing with the *causes* – that is, politicians and political parties themselves, and their propensity to drive politics into faction.[13]

One aspect of this is inevitable. Political parties come into being to pursue a set of interests, and that will involve opposing what they regard as contrary to those interests. Could this be prevented? Yes – by having a single political party in the state, populated by highly benevolent and altruistic individuals. Is this a plausible answer? Obviously not. There are plenty of one-party states in which this is claimed to be the case. Propaganda tells the people that the Party (think China) or the dictator (think North Korea) is the avuncular and kindly guardian of the people's welfare. But we are discussing what the concept of *democracy* entails in these matters, so a defence of this questionable alternative, if one is possible, can be left to the likes of Kim Jong-un and others.

However, reference to benevolence and altruism prompts a thought – not that there should be some way of ensuring that politicians exemplify both virtues, though that would be agreeable, but rather that two expectations should be imposed which produce something of the same effect. These are that those licensed by the enfranchised to take an active part in political life as legislators or office holders in government should bear scrutiny regarding their qualifications for the role, and should be held to the highest standards of duty in the role. Another way of putting the point is that engagement in politics and government should be seen as a service, not a career, and that the endeavours expected of someone in the fiduciary role of servant of the people and the state should not submerge that responsibility under considerations of his or her career.

Subordinating service to career is, alas but quite openly, standard behaviour in the British political system, despite the unequivocal requirements of the Code of Conduct laid down by the House of Commons for sitting MPs.[14] The Code (reproduced in full as Appendix IV) requires of MPs that they display 'selflessness, integrity, objectivity, accountability, openness, honesty and leadership', and specifies some of their duties thus (my italics): '6. Members have a general duty to act *in the interests of the nation as a whole*; and a special duty to their constituents. 7. Members should act on all occasions in accordance with *the public trust placed in them*. They should always behave with probity and integrity, including in their use of public resources.' The fiduciary role of service is emphasized: '11. Members shall base their conduct on a consideration of *the public interest*, avoid *conflict between personal interest and the public interest* and resolve any conflict between the two, *at once, and in favour of the public interest.'*

Yet MPs standardly and openly violate this code. They vote according to the party whip, whatever their personal view or judgment might be. Loyalty to the party interest, whether or not it is aligned with the national interest, is expected of MPs by their party machines, and dereliction is punished. They vote as instructed by the whips, whatever their own view or judgment, because not to do so threatens their career prospects. Opposing the party line might result in their not being supported by the party at the next election, thus losing their jobs. They might not be considered for preferment in the party hierarchy, or for ministerial office, as punishment or because they are regarded as 'unreliable' in party terms. Failure to serve the party's interests is one of the most serious political crimes a Member of Parliament can commit. They therefore rarely do it.[15] Which is to say: they rarely observe the requirements of the Code of Conduct.

An indignant MP might claim in response that voting the party line is indeed in the national interest, because his party line is in the national interest. Asking us to accept that his party is infallibly right about matters of policy, and always unequivocally acts in the national interest therefore, is asking a lot. But one can cite a clear historical example in which hundreds of MPs voted as their party required but which was not in the national interest, as made clear by published objective assessments by the government of the day – a government that happened to be drawn from the selfsame party that whipped a vote *against* what its own economic assessments showed was the right policy. This was during the Brexit process, in which the most optimistic assessment of the impact on the UK economy of leaving the EU showed a serious downturn with consequent negative impact on employment rates, earnings, investment, and provision of public services. It cannot be held in the national interest for this to happen, least of all as an act of deliberate and avoidable policy. War or other external and unavoidable factors might make such a thing happen. But in this case the members of the governing party were whipped to vote in favour of it happening. And almost every one of them did.[16]

Moreover, reference in the Code of Conduct to the duty of MPs to serve 'the interests of the nation as a whole' and 'the public interest' is consistently violated by MPs who refuse to engage with members of the public if they are not voters in their own constituencies. In doing this MPs who pass laws affecting the whole nation are refusing to engage with the majority of people impacted by their doing so. Hiding behind the 'tradition' that MPs deal with *local problems of constituents only* is a convenient way of avoiding the larger responsibility of the national interest. MPs are members *of Parliament*, and Parliament's responsibility is to the state and its citizens *as a whole*; it follows that all voters are entitled to question any MP, because MPs are answerable to the public. Their salaries, their expenses, and the expenses of Parliament do not come exclusively from their constituents' taxes, nor is it only their constituents whose taxes pay for the policies they vote to implement. The standard practice of avoiding engagement with the majority of people whom they govern is a violation of the Code.

MPs use the ambiguity of the choice they can make between national and local roles as a convenience. It helps when, say, a given MP's constituency voted in a referendum for a nationally damaging proposition which she knows to be so, allowing her to defend her subsequent actions either way: positioning herself as a mandatory of her constituents, obliged to vote in Parliament as they did in her constituency, or, if she chooses to vote the other way in Parliament, positioning herself as a servant of the national interest despite what her constituents chose. She might vote as her constituents did wholly or in part because she fears that doing otherwise might damage her chances of re-election. In this case, she votes in her self-interest, not in that of her constituents or the nation, and therefore again in violation of the Code.

These are matters of common knowledge and observation. So is the fact that the House of Commons Code of Conduct is both drawn up and policed by the House of Commons itself. The old question *quis custodiet ipsos custodes?* (who watches the watchmen?) arises here. The Code is exemplary; it should not be too difficult to enforce it upon 650 Members of Parliament; yet the factional activities of the party machines, and the careerism and political tribalism displayed by MPs, are only part of the story. Recurrent scandals over MPs' misuse of public funds in, for example, expenses claims, failure to enter perks and outside earnings in the Register of Interests, relationships with lobbies, and the 'revolving door' phenomenon of ex-MPs and ex-ministers taking high-salaried positions with commercial interests with which they had been connected while in office, all point to a system which does not consistently rise to the level that the Code of Conduct sets, and is insufficiently policed given that it polices itself.

How familiar are voters with the Code of Conduct? How many have read it? Do they test candidates and MPs against its requirements, either in the selection process by asking whether the track record of a candidate suggests a likelihood of compliance with the Code if elected, or in assessing the track record of a current MP regarding actual compliance? A reasonable guess is that this is extremely rare. Candidates are proposed by party machines on grounds that suit the party; party activists, a tiny minority of voters in a constituency, influence the adoption of candidates on grounds that include ideological suitability and purity of party allegiance. The sheer numbers of MPs, only a moiety of whom can hope to succeed in achieving ministerial office at some level, let alone the heights of cabinet appointment or the Prime Ministership itself, are in effect parliamentary lobby fodder, and what the party requires of them is that they are agreeable to voters so that they can be elected, and, once in Parliament, loyal so that they will unquestioningly vote the party line. Loyalty is thus far more important than independent judgment, if this latter is important at all.

As these considerations show, there is a point at which the quality of candidates for positions of public trust can be interrogated by the public itself. In an ideal democracy voters would scrutinize the fitness of candidates, explore their credentials, evaluate their experience, intelligence, and past actions, and listen carefully to their responses to questions about all these matters. If voters do not do this, so a severe critic would say, they get the representatives they deserve.

There are those who defend (most) MPs as individuals, blaming the dysfunctionality of the institution of Parliament, the unreasonableness of voters, and the complexity and difficulty of politics itself, for most of their failings, redescribing the failings as frustrations instead.[17] The first and third of these points are good ones: Parliament is an archaic and dysfunctional institution, loaded in favour of the sitting government, and politics is hard, as evidenced by the fact that all political careers end in failure, unless a politician leaves the game early (by choice or the assassin's bullet: think of John F. Kennedy) while still popular. But the events of 2019 in the British Parliament, when the degree of control exercised by the whipping system of party discipline largely broke down because the government was in the minority and the policy questions facing Parliament were bitterly divisive in ways that cut across party lines, threw a strong and exceedingly unflattering light on the degree to which MPs' actions were governed by their Code of Conduct.

The process by which candidates for the Presidency of the United States are selected would seem to be exactly the kind of exhaustive evaluation of fitness suggested by the foregoing. The long and gruelling path through primaries and caucuses by which a presidential candidate seeks nomination by his or her party, and the election campaign itself, is certainly a test of mental and physical robustness – but also perhaps, as appears in the case of the Trump phenomenon, of a certain pachydermous insensibility on the candidate's part. It is a test also of the candidate's track record, private life, past utterances, and the detail of his or her political inclinations and alliances.[18] This can be viewed as the endeavour to sift and test whether the candidate is 'in an eminent degree endowed with the requisite qualifications', to use Hamilton's words. But Hamilton himself did not think voters would do this, nor that such a judgment could reliably emerge from the Babel of political and journalistic vilification or hagiography, dependent on party allegiance, that would take the place of evaluation in the public debate. That is why he proposed the Electoral College, intended to be a jury of wise, sober, and neutral minds that would assess the candidate's fitness for high and demanding office.

Hamilton's doing this was a mark of his scepticism both about voters and the public debate mediated by the press. Indeed it was more: it was a mark of the general Platonic scepticism that the Founders had about democracy itself, which is why only the House of Representatives is constituted by popular vote – and even then, undemocratically by the FPTP system, as chapter 2 showed – for the Senate represents the number of the States not the numerousness of voters in them, and the Presidency is elected by the indirect means of the parties-controlled Electoral College, not always reflecting the popular choice: neither George W. Bush nor Donald Trump won majorities of the popular vote in their elections to the White House.

This layering of filters exists in the American system because its designers did not believe, and their successors still do not do so, that the enfranchised can be relied upon to be careful enough about whom they select, nor that party activists can be relied upon to be dispassionate enough to present candidates to the enfranchised who are 'qualified in an eminent degree' for the task they are to undertake. If voters were more engaged and careful, and if the influence of activists and donors of money were not so great, the chances of representatives being of better quality, and of their being adequately held to the standards set for service in positions of public trust, would be greater, and the need for these kinds of filters less.

Three considerations suggest how voters could become more careful about whom they choose. One is if they know that their votes really count, so that they know that participating makes a difference. To repeat, as one endlessly must: FPTP systems effectively disenfranchise large numbers, often indeed the majority, of voters, making them feel that participating is futile. Many therefore do not participate. The ping-pong battle of the two-party system produced by FPTP voting is not responsive to the choice made by the individual at the ballot box. In the US not much more than a third of the adult voting age population participates in mid-term congressional elections, and not much more than half in presidential elections, in large part because of this. That is scandalous; non-participation is itself a corruption of democracy.

Greater participation might also weaken the influence of activists on candidate selection. This would be beneficial because representatives who owe their position to a group of activists in their constituency or congressional district are more likely to place the party interest (which means their own career interest) above any other, including the national interest, when conflicts of interest arise.

An allied point is that in elections voters are presented with party manifestos, containing a raft of policies bundled together on a take-it-all-or-leave-it basis. To vote for a candidate is to vote for the whole package offered by the party. A major result is that where voters do not choose someone for her known and liked personal qualities – which sometimes happens – they vote for the party label because of the overall preference they have for the *kind* of things they take that party to stand for. It is safe to venture that careful examination of individual manifesto policies is not the norm in most households at election time. A few bullet points as presented in the media would make the standard sum of what voters know. There is no obvious remedy to having manifestos at election time, despite the inherent evil of parties being able to smuggle in highly partisan policy proposals or unobviously undesirable commitments beneath a camouflage of popular-seeming ideas, and despite the likelihood that they will not be properly scrutinized by the mass of voters. But the more voters feel they can make a difference – that their votes actually count – the more likely they are to take notice.

This leads to the second consideration, relating to the quality of voters as voters. Imagine a situation in which a major and continuous theme of high school education relates to the forthcoming responsibilities of being a voter. Knowledge of the electoral and parliamentary or congressional systems, frequent practical activity of hustings and voting in school, and public recognition of the significance of reaching voting age, would prepare young people for the responsibility. There is a strong case for the voting age to be set at sixteen, as argued in chapter 2. Early participation in the political process, especially in the context of explicit preparation for it, has a chance of fostering not just participation but more thoughtful participation, especially if conjoined with an electoral system where all votes always make a difference.

The third consideration is the availability of reliable information. This brings into view a matter of major significance in democracy, and I discuss it below. At this juncture it suffices to say that the quality of outcome of votes cast has a chance of being enhanced if voters are informed and aware, and therefore more confident that their choices are well-grounded.

The election of Donald Trump as President of the US in 2016 is evidence of the need for improvements such as these. To put the point at its most neutral, writing as an outside observer, and granting all the negatives that could be imputed on both sides of the 2016 presidential election campaign, there is no question but that the balance of knowledge and experience required for adequate performance of the presidential role lay, by a very large margin, with Hillary Clinton. No rational calculation of which of the two candidates had the better credentials for that office could result in the opposite view. To put the point at its most polemical: Hillary Clinton had been a practising lawyer, a two-term President's wife, a senator, and a Secretary of State. In terms of qualification and experience, leaving aside questions of personality, she was a highly plausible presidential candidate. Donald Trump widely attracted description – and not only by extreme political opponents – as a bloviating, narcissistic, unintelligent, incontinent, foolhardy, and ignorant individual, born rich, with experience limited to real estate and television, and with views on race and a record of treatment of women which were both, at the least, problematic. This should have been enough to call his fitness for office into question at an early stage of the electoral process. It did not; and this is an indictment of a system supposedly intended to ensure persons 'qualified in an eminent degree' for high office. It certainly demonstrates that if ever the situation of political restraint envisaged by Levitsky and Ziblatt obtained, by then it had ceased to do so.

The warning sign about the health of US democracy that is the election of Donald Trump is paralleled by the warning sign about the health of British democracy that is Brexit. Recall that a referendum on membership of the European Union was called by Conservative Prime Minister David Cameron expressly as a means of silencing the 'Eurosceptics' on the right wing of his party. The Eurosceptic group had existed since the accession of the United Kingdom to the European Economic Community in 1973, and it had not been silenced by a referendum in 1975 yielding a substantial majority in favour of membership. Its disruptive presence in periods of Conservative government had been a cause of difficulty for successive Conservative Prime Ministers, one of whom, Sir John Major, famously expressed public irritation with its members in what is known as 'unparliamentary language'.[19] The referendum called by David Cameron was held in June 2016.

Despite controversy over the question of the franchise for the 2016 referendum, a simple general election franchise was used. It had been argued that everyone with a material interest in the outcome should be given a voice, as in the Scottish Independence Referendum of 2014 which included everyone aged sixteen and upwards, and citizens of other EU countries living and working in Scotland. For the 2016 referendum a case was made to fulfil a promise to re-enfranchise British expatriates of longer than fifteen years' standing. However, all three groups were denied a voice. On the grounds that the referendum was advisory only, no threshold or supermajority requirement was imposed. In the event, 37% of the electorate for the referendum voted in favour of leaving the European Union. This represented 51.89% of votes cast on the day, in raw numbers 17.41 million out of a population of 65.65 million. Thus, just over a third of the electorate, consisting of just over a quarter of the population, voted for the 'Leave' option.

Parliament chose to regard this as mandating an exit from the European Union. Neither the advisory-only referendum itself nor the proportion of the electorate that voted for 'Leave' can by any standards be regarded as providing such a mandate, but in the campaign beforehand the then Prime Minister David Cameron had pledged to abide by the outcome, therefore creating a 'political' mandate. It became a trope among many politicians that the outcome of 51.89% of votes cast therefore had to be 'respected', although criminal offences were found by the Electoral Commission to have been committed by the 'Leave' campaigns, which would have voided the outcome if the referendum had *not* been advisory only.[20]

Because questions about constitutionality are discussed in chapter 6, it is relevant, as necessary background, to enrich these points about the Brexit referendum with the following observation. The fact that the referendum was advisory only follows from the doctrine of parliamentary sovereignty.[21] In preparation for discussion in the House of Commons of the bill for the referendum, the House of Commons Library Briefing Paper No. 07212 (3 June 2015) explicitly set out for MPs in its §5 the fact of the referendum's advisory nature, and reminded them in §6 that, if they were minded to consider the outcome as mandating, a threshold or supermajority should be stipulated.

This was re-emphasized in the House of Commons on 16 June 2015, in the debate on the referendum bill, by the then

Minister for Europe David Lidington, who asserted on the record that no threshold or supermajority was required because the referendum was advisory only.[22] The decision to treat the outcome as politically mandating accordingly impugns the undertakings explicitly embodied in the information given to MPs in their Briefing Paper and in the Minister's words on the floor of the House. Every aspect of this – the sovereignty point, the status of the referendum, the fact that it would have been voided if non-advisory because of illegalities in the procurement of the 'Leave' vote, the absence of a threshold or supermajority bar, and the fact that the small majority of votes cast represented a mere 37% of the total electorate – raises serious questions of constitutional propriety and principle.

Parliament should be the place where such points are taken into careful consideration. They were never discussed there. Had they been examined there, and had considerations about the economic impact on the national interest been conjoined with them, it would have been inconsistent with the Parliamentary Code of Conduct for MPs to vote in ways that treated the outcome of the 2016 Brexit referendum as safe. The Brexit example therefore casts serious doubt on the fitness for purpose of the party system, the electoral system that produces and sustains it, and the quality of those elected in it. It also raises questions about the constitutional safeguards that were manifestly lacking in allowing a great and consequential constitutional change to be 'mandated' by 37% of a restricted electorate. On this latter point see chapter 6.

Much that has so far been said turns on voters having access to full and accurate information, together with sober and impartial analysis of it, to help them in choosing how to vote. The first point to be acknowledged is that large swathes of the population simply do not care much about politics, except perhaps briefly at election times or, individually, when something happens that personally affects them. Alas, provision of fully detailed, clear, and accurate information is more likely to have the adverse effect of turning them away rather than engaging and empowering them. Campaigners know two crucial things: that sentiment or emotion is more likely than reason to drive choice in the ballot box, as it does in most other matters; and that attention spans are short. Political advertising is therefore a matter of slogans designed on the basis of these two facts. Slogans are only in a tenuous sense information; they are certainly not analysis.

That, to repeat, has to be acknowledged. But there are still newspapers and magazines, and there are the social media. What of these? The first problem here is that newspapers have to make a profit to survive. Familiarly, 'what interests the public' is frequently more interesting to the public than 'the public interest', and to sell themselves newspapers have to act accordingly. Celebrity adultery and royal babies easily outdo taxation policy in this regard. Serious newspapers and magazines have small readerships and find it hard to survive. When larger-circulation newspapers push their owners' political line, they do as the campaigners do: they rely on slogans, or at most very brief and partisan – and thus, in particular, non-analytic – editorializing. The traditional press overall, its small 'serious' corner excepted, has ceased to be a reliable source of information, and indeed has become a destabilizing force, as witness the relentless misrepresentation-based xenophobia and aggressive political partisanship of the three (out of four) largest-circulation tabloid newspapers in Britain, all owned by what bankers call 'ultra-high net worth individuals' who do not reside in the UK.

Social media have taken over as the main conduits of information, opinion, and debate in most countries in the world. On the one hand, cyberspace reprises the agora of old; it is a market-place of ideas and views, a free democracy of debate. Alas, the positive aspects contend with, and generally speaking are drowned out by, the negative aspects: hate speech, falsehood, and polemic. The quantum of falsehood, and very often its nature – the skill with which it is presented – corrupts the entire field of information, making it extremely difficult to disentangle reliable from false information.

In the UK the public service broadcaster, the BBC, exists – according to its charter – to provide accurate news with impartial, accurate, and thoughtful exploration of its implications. Let us acknowledge and leave aside the fact that the BBC is a world-beater in drama and documentary programming. Its news service once shared the same reputation. However, its standing as a news service was seriously damaged by editorial decisions taken in response to the 2016 Brexit referendum and the line thus established in the subsequent years of debate on the matter. Put at its simplest, the decision was taken to treat the referendum outcome as having settled the matter of UK membership of the EU, and subsequent treatment of questions relating to the Brexit process were predicated on 'when, not if' the UK would quit the EU. Accordingly those who campaigned to reverse the decision were treated as marginal to the main debate, which focused instead on the variety of competing positions taken as to what Brexit meant and how it should happen.[23] A substantial drop in audiences of the news service followed, not unexpectedly given the circumstances of extremely deep division over the matter in the country as a whole. As soon as a news service is seen to be biased, it loses credibility, and serves only to reinforce the prejudices and bolster the beliefs of those on the same side.

The loss of a reliable and impartial source of information and discussion makes it necessary to reinvent the process. It cannot be a profit-supported process because it would not survive as such: it has to be publicly funded. It therefore requires to be immunized against any form of political or partisan pressure also. A suggestion might be as follows. There already exist in the UK bodies charged with duties to be performed in the public interest, such as the National Audit Office which scrutinizes government spending on behalf of Parliament. Just such a body charged with checking the factuality of news, information, and claims made in the course of public expressions of opinion and party-political assertions, and which publishes its findings, would be a major boon to society. All the more so if the method of publishing its findings had wide reach – easily achieved by requiring all online, print, and broadcast forums to carry reports of its findings as a condition of their licences. To preserve the freedom of these media otherwise, they should be allowed to say what they like in commentary on the findings: but the findings should be out in the public domain.

The idea of *audit* can be made to apply more generally. It was noted above that the Parliamentary Standards Committee maintains oversight of MPs' behaviour. Although the public hears of such cases as questionable expenses claims and failure to register outside interests, one never hears of the Committee complaining that any MP has failed to conform to the Code of Conduct in respect of failing to act in the national interest, or putting her self-interest above the public interest. An independent body outside Parliament that subjects MPs' activities to scrutiny in light of the Code of Conduct, and publishes its findings, would do a great service likewise.

So too would a more direct audit of legislators' engagement with their duties. Persistent spot checks on legislators' knowledge of the detail of bills they are to vote on would be an excellent way of ensuring that they are fulfilling their duty to the people and the state. The very least that can be expected of them is a good knowledge of the legislation they vote on. In all other walks of life performance is monitored and evaluated as a condition of employment; there is every reason to do likewise in the legislature. This could be made to apply in any parliamentary system now. But note that in an institutional separation of legislative and executive functions, legislators' entire time would be devoted to the scrutiny, evaluation, challenge, and correction of legislation, and would very particularly be based on a presumption of diligence in the execution of that function.

This latter is just one thought relating to the general question of changes that can be made to improve the quality and efficacy of legislators. The following are, arguably, equally if not more advisable.

If there were a clear separation of powers between legislature and executive, effected by the location of these powers in distinct institutions, one aspect of the careerism that compels so many MPs in parliamentary systems to place party loyalty above national interest, when these conflict, would be ended. If being a legislator does not lead to being a minister or Prime Minister, that will remove one powerful incentive to assiduous obedience to a party line, namely, hope of preferment. On the other hand, if legislators' membership of Select Committees was rewarded with ministerial-level salaries, this would be a worthwhile career incentive. Select Committees hold ministers and government officials to account, and if these committees had real powers, including powers of subpoena and sanction, membership of them would be a highly worthwhile aim for any politician wishing to make both government and her country better.

The whipping system is highly questionable. One way to reduce the power of whips over individual legislators is to make voting by legislators secret. When an electronic voting system is at last introduced to the archaic British Parliament, secret voting will be easy – and, unlike the situation at this time of writing, quick: a gain over the current laborious method of physically walking past tellers in a lobby to record a vote. The drawback to secret ballots in Parliament is that the voting record of MPs would not be available to the electors in their constituencies. So the question arises whether losing the whip-observed transparency of voting in Parliament is more or less an addition to democracy than loss of the voter-observed voting record. The concept of a *representative* democracy gives the answer to this dilemma. An MP is not a mandatory or mere delegate of her electors, but a representative, sent with plenipotentiary powers to get information, listen and contribute to debate, make decisions, and act on them – in the best interests of her country and constituents. Accordingly the *independence* of her judgment and choice in Parliament is key. Her vote there should not be controlled by the party whips and should therefore be secret.

A different method by which legislators can be rendered independent of both party control and career ambitions is a cap on the amount of time they can serve as a legislator. If a person can occupy a seat in Parliament for only one term, there is no re-election pressure or career consideration for him to do anything other than vote his judgment. Capping terms would be neither so needful nor indeed so attractive an option where executive and legislature are separate, for here the accumulation of experience on legislative committees would be an advantage. Having legislators sitting on the 'backbenches' of the legislature, who never do anything else for many repeated terms, standardly voting the party line, is a waste of democratic opportunity. It is too much the current norm – and indeed always has been – in the British Parliament.

In circumstances of a fully democratic electoral system but without separation of executive from legislature, the great likelihood is that governments will consist of coalitions. In these circumstances the independence of the legislative vote is both an advantage and a disadvantage. The advantage is that measures brought before the legislature have to stand or fall on their merits in the view of a sufficient number of legislators from different political standpoints. The disadvantage is that a coalition partner pledged to allow another partner's legislation through, in return for passage of its own legislation, must be able to deliver its support; and that requires marshalling its legislators to vote accordingly. Again, however, the concept of *democracy* itself provides the answer. It is better for legislation to have the approval of a majority in the diversity of political standpoints in a legislature than that legislators should obediently vote in line with party considerations, if these latter diverge from the merits of the legislation.

By far the most attractive option is to separate the executive and legislature, and to take measures both to increase the independence of legislators and to incentivize their active participation in scrutinizing the executive's actions and holding it to account. Until those systems are reformed in which the executive is drawn from the majority in the legislature, diminishing the power of the party system over individual legislators is highly necessary. Add to either of these points the idea of a proportional electoral system which engages more considered participation by more voters, not only in the polling booth but in choosing their representatives and observing their subsequent performance – thus diminishing the influence of activists while raising the standards of those elected to serve – and manifold improvements come into view. Add further the wide availability of impartial fact-checking on the Babel of claims, opinions, and campaign exhortations, and the improvement is yet greater.

A final point that merits mention concerns two other bodies of people in the political and governmental system and their contrasting influence. One is the Civil Service, consisting of the people who implement the executive function of government. Senior civil servants work closely with ministers, advising them about how to put their policies into effect. Their conditions of employment require a scrupulous separation between their private political inclinations and their work. The other body of people, far less numerous, consists of the party-political advisors in the private offices of legislators and ministers. Whereas civil servants are employed as a result either or both of examinations or open employment competition, advisors are political appointees. They are neither elected nor appointed by an open and transparent process; almost all are unknown to the public, as therefore are their qualifications and experience for the role of advising people whose activities will impact the public. The only thing one can be sure about them is that they have, from the point of view of their employers, the right ideological stance for the role they perform. Advisors tend to be ambitious to become legislators themselves, and embed themselves in the party system to achieve the approval of their seniors. Party loyalty starts early; the careerist imperatives are in the blood from the outset. Madison's view of factionalism was that it is inbred in human nature; it is certainly in the DNA of *homo politicus*.[24]

There is complete clarity of expectation about the role of civil servants, because there is transparency about their appointment and conditions of service. Given the fiduciary nature of political office, the very least that might be demanded of a holder of such office is that all those upon whom she relies in her work should be publicly identified: the names, qualifications, and experience of her political advisors should be open to public view so that if electors or others had reservations about the influence their representative was under, they could be expressed.

And the point generalizes. Who sponsors a legislator for election? Who is donating campaign funds, and how much? What is the standing and the agenda of sponsors and financers? These points supplement what should anyway be standard questions for electors about those standing for election – their qualifications and experience, their track record, and their stated commitments.

These thoughts are instances of a general principle of democracy: that transparency and accountability are inseparable from it. Democracy cannot exist in shadows, nor even have its roots in them.

5

GOVERNANCE AND CONSTITUTIONALITY

In his discussion of factionalism – party divisions – Madison argued that if you cannot prevent its causes, you can limit the harm of its effects.[1] As we have just seen, one way of doing so is to interrogate the question of the *personnel* of politics – those who stand for election, who seek government posts, who drive debate and party policy decisions as activists. No doubt many people enter politics with high motives, wishing to serve their fellow citizens and to make their countries and societies better. But it is as well to accept that ambition, careerism, the relentless pressures of political and governmental reality, compromises, and subordination to the demands of party loyalty can tarnish the brightest of early hopes.

The facts of factionalism, and the pressures of political life, together therefore prompt an additional set of thoughts, this time about the *institutional* arrangements required to ensure that the purposes of government are achieved despite the variability of the human material that occupies the seats of legislation and execution in government. Remembering Han Fei's farmer, we are wise not to expect too many noble-minded, gifted, self-sacrificing statesmen and stateswomen to emerge and thenceforth govern with inclusivity, compassion, vision, and genius. Alas. For that reason, and with due apologies to those politicians who genuinely wish they could display these virtues – and who even try – the legislative and executive institutions of state have to be designed for the lowest common denominator. The institutions have to be rule-governed and transparent, they have to be independently audited for effectiveness, their personnel have to be fully accountable for the offices they hold – and regularly held to such account. So much is obvious.

But the thought this in turn prompts is Kafka's Castle: a mindless bureaucracy, formulaic, insensitive, operated by 'jobsworths' who crank the handle merely. It is intrinsic to numerously staffed hierarchies that those in the middle and lower ranks of the structure have limited or no discretion, are under instruction to apply the rules, and are sanctioned for failure to do so. It is obviously right that this too should be so, because the purposes for which the institution exists would be foiled otherwise.

How is the dilemma thus identified best mitigated?

The answer lies in the way the institutions of government themselves are constituted in light of their purpose. In a democracy the legislative and executive institutions, by definition of the word 'democracy', exist to serve the interests of the people, and though there will always be political differences about what those interests are and – even more so – how they are to be served, there are certain fundamentals that no institution can be allowed to fail to deliver. The implementation of policies that make the people as a whole, or the already less-well-off sections of them, poorer, or which reduce their rights, or which remove access to decent basic health care, education, and amenities such as potable water and clean air is manifestly not *for the people*, and the people would not agree to such policies given an opportunity for rational consideration of their effects, except in circumstances of emergency such as war or major disaster. The *for the people* constraint is the principal test of the health of the institutions of government, and entails that their operation should not be *for the interests of one side of the political divide only* or *for one section of society only*. This reprises a central theme of this book: *in the good state, government transcends politics*. The good state is a democracy in the entailed meaning of this word.

The question now is how the institutions of state are to be constituted so that they serve this democratic purpose.

In a democracy there can be no question of proscribing anyone from standing for election or office, except in extreme circumstances of unfitness. It is the responsibility of electors to decide whether they think someone is a fit person to do the important job of representing them. As previously shown, too often candidates are imposed on electors by party machines or by a small group of activists, and electors vote as often, if not more so, for a party label rather than a person. They rarely scrutinize candidates for genuine ability and suitability, leaving others to do their choosing for them – too often on grounds of party loyalty, ideological purity, or both.

That concerns the informal – people – side of the equation. From the formal – institutional – side of the equation there is much that can be done to keep legislators and executives up to the mark. A suggestion made in the previous chapter is that an independent commission should audit legislators' work performance. Continuous performance monitoring is standard in many areas of business and education, and in the crucial work of legislation ought to be standard likewise. One method of doing so is by monitoring attendance and interrogating legislators' knowledge of the bills they are debating. It is highly probable that if such a system were introduced suddenly and without warning, the majority of legislators would be found in an unacceptable state of ignorance or unclarity about the detail of bills under consideration before them.

Such a commission would already have the powers of monitoring compliance with standards in public life, as now. Its advantage would be its independence; the legislature would not be its own judge and jury.

It is a responsibility of government to evaluate the need for, and the cost and impact of, legislation it proposes. In systems where government is drawn from a political party which has won its side of a disagreement over public policy matters, and controls the majority of *seats* in the legislature therefore, while other parties – perhaps between them representing a majority of the *electorate* – oppose their view, it is inevitable that the government will claim justification for its legislation on the grounds that it has a mandate for it, although in resisting criticism it will also of course claim that it has properly evaluated the need for the legislation and its cost and impact. But only in the case of fully bipartisan legislation would such a claim be uncontentious. Because both the proposal and opposition to it are typically based on party-political lines, the public would be well served by a non-partisan assessment of the need, cost, and likely impact of legislation. An independent commission publishing the results of such assessment would provide a crucial public service. If it also evaluated the effects of previous legislation on the same basis, so that its remit was, Janus-faced, to examine both the likely future effect of current legislation, and the actual effect of past legislation, the value of its service would be all the greater.

In a system where the independent audit of proposed and existing legislation was a standard public service, it would be wise for legislation to include, as standard, a sunset clause – a dated limit to the period of its application – so that if it is found wanting in its effects its lapsing or revision is already mandated.

Constraints such as these would have a very salutary effect on the proposing and drafting of legislation, which would have to pass the scrutiny of such a tribune whose work is independent of party-political purpose. To the objection that an unelected body would thus be mandated to pass judgment on what elected legislators propose, one can give the following two replies. First, there is no suggestion that such a body should have the power to strike down legislation. If the legislature wished to proceed with passing into law provisions that the independent body found wanting, they could; electors would pass the final judgment on their doing so. Second, any body constituted by the legislature – the elected representatives of the people – has a democratic mandate thereby. A scrutiny tribune set up to evaluate the impact of legislation would have just such a mandate.

The foregoing suggestions are consistent either with a parliamentary system, where government is drawn from a majority in the legislature, or the far better system of separated powers, where the legislative and executive functions are exercised by distinct institutions. However, given the dangers inherent in a parliamentary system from careerism, party control of individual representatives, and the executive's near-automatic control in securing passage of its legislation because the legislature is its creature, more is needed.

One suggestion already made is the imposition of term limits, restricting a legislator to serving one or anyway a limited number of terms only. If the restriction is to a single term, the pressure of trying to ensure re-election vanishes, and with it careerist motives and the power of party whips. The argument against restricted terms is that the experience and insight gained by good legislators would be wasted. In a system of sortition, legislators appointed by lottery would serve restricted terms; any argument against the idea of limited terms is an argument against this system also. The need for limiting representatives' terms would be far less, if applicable at all, in a separated system where legislators are devoted solely to the business of legislation and are barred from membership of the executive, as in the US; here accumulated experience would not be wasted.

The practices and procedures of almost all legislatures in developed countries are complex, and in some – like the British Parliament – archaic and cumbersome, the archaism serving the majority party's advantage because it controls the processes of debate – including *what* is debated; opposition parties have restricted opportunities to initiate debates – and timing of legislation. Due process is of course a necessity; time for proper consideration and debate is essential, review by a second chamber (more on this shortly) is highly desirable, and when intelligent forms of procedure are laid down and correctly followed, they provide assurance that the process is lawful and proper. But processes can be so complex that they lack transparency. As with the requirement that justice needs to be seen to be done, so the legislative process needs to be transparent to public observation.

Almost all developed political orders have bicameral legislatures, the second chamber constituted on a basis different from the first chamber. The norm is for the second chamber to be elected on a different franchise, or to be appointed. The US Senate and the British House of Lords provide respective examples. A standard argument against elected second chambers is that they constitute an alternative locus of democratically authorized power, threatening paralysis if the two chambers disagree. A standard argument against appointed second chambers is that they are undemocratic because unelected.

This latter point is incorrect; as already noted, many of the organs of governance, such as (to take the British example) the Civil Service, the Audit Commission, and any number of 'quangos' (quasi-governmental organizations appointed for specific tasks), are unelected, but because they exist on the authority of the elected legislature and government they are *ipso facto* part of the democratic order.

A second chamber appointed as a reviewing and revising chamber, without the degree of legislative authority of the directly elected chamber, is as democratic as the latter. It does however have to be suitably constituted. To continue with the British example: if the criteria for membership of the House of Lords were specialist expertise and representation of minorities, geographical regions, and sectors of the economy, and if it had (as is indeed the case) very weak or no powers, authorized only to suggest improvements to legislation or to propose needed legislation for the representative house to take up, it would provide an extremely useful source of perspective. To a considerable extent the House of Lords achieves this purpose, despite having, at time of writing, too many retired party politicians and – still – hereditary members. The 'cross-bench' peers, those appointed without party affiliation, are the model of what all members of the House of Lords should be: not party-political, but appointed for their expertise and experience, thus possessed of qualifications that genuinely contribute to good legislation and governance.

The US Senate manages to capture the worst of both defects of the House of Lords: its members are party-political, and yet it is unrepresentatively elected. Its original *raison d'être* was to ensure that the interests of small, low-population states are not overwhelmed by the interests of large-population states. It frequently succeeds in achieving Republican majorities because small, unpopulous rural states tend to be conservative while states with large populations tend to have higher proportions of liberal-minded voters. These latter are effectively disenfranchised in a system which makes the vote of a small-state voter equal to a considerable number of votes in a large state. This is 'plural voting' with a vengeance.

If the British system should reform itself into an American system in which the legislative and executive functions reside in different institutions, then the American system should reform itself into the British system of a Senate of expertise, experience, and sectoral representation by non-party-political appointment. That would require some revision to other aspects of the US's constitutional arrangements, because of the intricate interrelationship of the Senate's functions with so many aspects of the political order. But one of the recurrent features of US politics in its two-party form – courtesy of the undemocratic FPTP electoral system – is gridlock; the example is most publicly manifest in the frequently repeated failure of Congress and Presidency to agree a budget.

These and cognate suggestions are about making the institutional aspect of the political and governmental order serve the purposes of democracy. Lying behind the suggestions is a dominating thought: that the arrangements on which a democracy is based have to be transparent, consistent, well-ordered, and invulnerable to variation merely as a response to temporary political expedients. Developing and evolving the arrangements of a democracy to meet changing circumstances is itself something that needs to be done in an orderly and democratic way. What is needed for fulfilling the demands made by the concept of democracy is, in short, a *constitution* suitable for that purpose.

Once again, historical examples provide background. Consider the situation in France in the early months of 1793, following the execution of Louis XVI in January of that year, and the beginning of the 'Terror' in the following summer. In the previous autumn the king had been deposed and a republic declared; now the National Convention appointed a committee to draft a constitution for the new republic. One of its members, the mathematician and philosopher Nicolas de Condorcet (Marie Jean Antoine Nicolas de Caritat, Marquis de Condorcet, 1743–93), was the principal author of the first draft produced, but never adopted. Although politically neutral between the Jacobins and Girondins in the Convention – respectively the 'Left' and 'Right' in political terms – Condorcet's proposals were largely supported by the latter. After his condemnation following the Jacobin seizure of power under Robespierre, a different constitution was drafted and subsequently adopted, known as the 'Constitution of 1793'.

When Condorcet presented his draft to the Convention in February 1793 he had a sore throat and was unable to speak, so his colleague Bertrand Barère read out his proposals. In them Condorcet had tried to solve the perennial dilemma of democracy, namely, how 'to strike a balance between robust popular participation and the production of rational laws'. The ochlocracy of *sans-culottes* on the Paris streets was a pointed example of how 'robust popular participation' made 'the production of rational laws' difficult if not impossible.[2] Commenting on what he had read to the Convention, Barère remarked that 'a constitution expressly adopted by the citizens, and including the regular means of correcting and changing itself, is the only one by which a people, understanding their rights, jealous of preserving, after having lately recovered them, and still fearing they may be lost, can be subject to permanent order.'[3] Barère's reference to the turmoil current in the France of that moment can be translated into a general point: history teaches the need for a society to have arrangements in place to preserve the steadiness of good times into the difficulties of bad times so that these latter can be survived and overcome. A constitution provides for the steadiness of good times, and is the bulwark against the worst of bad times. That was the principle Condorcet was attempting to embody in a clear statement of the structure of the state and the rights of its citizens. Details of any historically or culturally conditioned constitution aside, this principle articulates the very point of having a constitution in the first place.

The constitutions of the United States of America and the United Kingdom stand at opposite ends of a polarity, the one fixed almost to the point of fossilization, the other uncodified, opaque, and labile to the point of vacuity. Examples that prove these points are respectively American gun laws and British referendums.

The US Constitution, adopted in 1789 and amended twenty-seven times, has the character of holy writ, sometimes defensibly so – as with the First Amendment rights of free speech, freedom of assembly, and entrenchment of secularism – and sometimes indefensibly so – as with the Second Amendment right to 'bear arms', an outstanding example of how a constitutional provision can subvert its *raison d'être* and do harm. In the case of the Second Amendment the harm consists in gun-caused fatalities amounting, at time of writing, to 40,000 per annum – 110 a day, nearly five an hour, about one every twelve minutes.

The text of the Second Amendment reads, 'A well-regulated Militia, being necessary to the security of a free State, the right of the people to keep and bear Arms, shall not be infringed.' The great debate over whether this was a right of individuals or a right for 'the people' to maintain a perpetually armed militia was settled in 2008 by a Supreme Court judgment in favour of the 'individual right' reading, reversing a 1939 Supreme Court decision that went the other 'collective right' way.[4]

The constitutional point that needs to be made about the Second Amendment concerns not just the intentions of its drafters, but more materially the fact that when it was adopted the 'arms' in question were muzzle-loading muskets. Today the arms bought by people who commit mass murders at schools and colleges include automatic assault weapons such as the AR-15 rifle. This weapon, which comes in a number of varieties, can be legally purchased at the age of eighteen in states where it is illegal to purchase any alcoholic drink, including beer, under the age of twenty-one. Enthusiastically described by the National Rifle Association (NRA) as 'America's rifle', it was used in the following recent massacres: the Sandy Hook Elementary School shooting in 2012 (in which 20 children aged six and seven years were killed), the San Bernardino shooting in 2015 (14 killed, 22 seriously injured), the Las Vegas shooting in 2017 (58 killed, 422 wounded), the Sutherland Springs church shooting in 2017 (26 killed, 22 injured), and the Stoneman Douglas High School shooting in 2018 (17 students and teachers killed, 17 injured). This is not an exhaustive list. The Columbine High School killing of ten students in 1999 prompted Michael Moore's film *Bowling for Columbine* (2002), which challenged American gun culture and therefore the tenability of the Second Amendment; it was a powerful indictment, but it changed nothing. Expressions of horror and sadness pour out on every occasion of the gratuitous loss of life to gun violence; yet the tragedies continue, and the Second Amendment stands.

This is an example of how a constitutional provision which is no longer fit for purpose is kept in being because it serves the interests of a powerful lobby able to thwart efforts to amend it.

The NRA argues that 'it is not guns that kill people but people who kill people', a claim whose spuriousness is immediately obvious when one ponders this: imagine two equally populous countries with equal numbers of murderous individuals in them. In one, it is fairly easy to get guns. In the other, there are no guns, so the murderous have to resort to knives and baseball bats. Consider the relative effectiveness of the means available to these murderers. It is hard to see how an individual with a knife could achieve what the mass murderer in Norway did in 2011, killing 69 young people in a shooting rampage at a Youth League summer camp, or what the mass murderer in Las Vegas achieved in 2017 in killing 58 people, or the mass murderer who shot to death 51 people in two mosques in Christchurch, New Zealand, in 2019.[5] (Among the five weapons used by this murderer was an AR-15 rifle.)

In short, permitted private gun ownership is in its effects a licence for murder. Compare the action of the Australians following the use of an AR-15-type weapon in the shooting at Port Arthur in Tasmania in 1996, in which 35 people were killed and 23 wounded; Australia imposed gun controls, banning private ownership of weapons with a capacity of more than five rounds.

The example of a constitutional provision that licenses gun ownership offers several lessons. The original framers of the amendment might have avoided the ambiguity of its wording, but they could not have foreseen the development of weapons technology that would render the amendment toxic even by the time Winchester repeater rifles and Colt.45 handguns were developed in the nineteenth century, not to mention the Gatling and Maxim machine guns, the former seeing service to deadly effect in the American Civil War, the latter a powerful adjunct to British imperialism at its height – and their descendants enabling the unbridled slaughter of the First World War.[6] In light of the veil behind which the future lies, a constitution has to specify means for responding adequately and sensibly to changing circumstances, striking the balance between being too easily altered because of political fashion or an episode of moral panic, and being too difficult to alter because lobbying can so politicize the question that the required consensus is hard to achieve. This latter is the case with the Second Amendment and the NRA's control of it. By now the unfitness of the Second Amendment is starkly apparent; opposition to it is not a political fashion or a moral panic. The cemeteries of America provide a quiet, massive witness to the need for change. The inability of the US constitution to respond is an indictment of it.

At the opposite end of the spectrum, and far worse, is the UK's 'unwritten' – more accurately, *uncodified* – constitution, consisting partly of statute and in significant part of conventions and traditions. It has been well said of the British constitution that it consists of 'understandings that no one understands'. The fault of a constitution that is as ambiguous and misty as this is that it is open to manipulation. This consideration is not merely theoretical. Here is a pertinent concrete example: the innovation of referendums in the UK.

Until 1973 referendums were not part of constitutional practice in the UK, given that they are inconsistent with the concept of representative democracy in general, and the original Westminster Model's own doctrine of parliamentary sovereignty in particular. But the major change portended by joining the then European Economic Community in 1973 caused such divisions within the governing party – the Labour Party – that its leader, Harold Wilson, decided to take the matter out of politicians' hands and put it to the people. On

5 June 1975 the people approved the change by 67% to 33% on a turnout of 64%.

Wilson was able to do this because of a precedent-breaking decision to hold a referendum in 1973 in Northern Ireland on whether it should reunite with the rest of Ireland or remain part of the UK. Until that point, great matters requiring non-partisan consideration outside the adversarial arena of politics were considered by specially appointed Royal Commissions, panels of representative experts who took their time to scrutinize options, take specialist advice, discuss and reflect, and then report their recommendations to Parliament. At times Royal Commissions were used as a way of kicking temporarily difficult topics into the long grass, so that when at last a report was submitted the matter would have gone cold or been forgotten. Since 1975 referendums have taken the place of Royal Commissions as ways of dealing with matters that a government, or Parliament as a whole, cannot or will not decide – even though in a representative system it is precisely Parliament's duty to do so.

Indeed, prior to 1973 referendums were regarded as unconstitutional and 'alien' to the system of representative democracy in the UK. Winston Churchill proposed holding a referendum in 1945 to see whether the people wished his coalition government to remain in office until Japan was defeated, but the Labour Party leader Clement Attlee, serving as Deputy Prime Minister in the war-time coalition, said, 'I could not consent to the introduction into our national life of a device so alien to all our traditions as the referendum which has only too often been the instrument of Nazism and Fascism.'[7]

Some think that referendums are *par excellence* instruments of democracy. To think this is to fail to see the force of arguments for *representative* democracy. The complexity of most matters to be decided and acted upon by government requires consideration, expert testimony, discussion, and judgment. That is why the enfranchised elect representatives – not delegates or messengers – to attend the legislature and to do a job of work on the electors' behalf: the work of getting the facts, exploring them, listening to argument, debating, and deciding on the course of action to be taken. Very simple matters that can be formulated as unambiguous questions admitting of yes–no answers are suitable for referendums; when complex matters of constitutional significance are at stake, a referendum has to be very fully prepared with copious opportunities for information and discussion beforehand, and full and accurate assessments of what would follow if a change were made. Switzerland is offered as the principal example of a democracy based on frequent referendums, but it proves instead to be an example of low turn-outs and conservative outcomes as the norm.

Worst of all, by their very nature referendums cannot reflect diversity and nuance of opinion, and therefore violate the demo-cratic principle of representation itself. Their utility as instru-ments of 'Nazism and Fascism', as Attlee put it – more generally, of populism – resides precisely in the crude character of binary options in response to necessarily simplistic questions.

There have been eleven referendums between 1973 and 2016 in the UK. Three of them have been on a nationwide basis (1975 on EEC membership, 2011 on proportional representation, 2016 on EU membership); most of the others were regional, mainly concerned with devolution of government powers to Scotland and Wales. Despite general provisions for the conduct of referendums in the Political Parties, Elections and Referendums Act 2000, relating to financial limitations and the duties of Counting Officers, there is no blueprint prescribing a consistent format for the conduct of referendums and a clear account of what will follow on their outcome. Technically, all referendums can only be advisory because Parliament is sovereign; this leaves it open that Parliament might or might not act on the outcome of a referendum depending on its degree of willingness in either direction. Parliament could decide to act in a manner contrary to a referendum result and legitimately claim that it was fulfilling its representative duty to act in the best interests of the country. Or a government in power could make a *political* undertaking to regard itself as mandated by an outcome to act one way or another, even though constitutionally it is not so obliged.

As a result there have been formal and informal inconsistencies in the way that referendums have been run and their outcomes treated. The referendum on devolution for Scotland in 1979 required a minimum threshold for a Yes vote of 40% of the electorate for devolution to happen; on the day of the vote a majority was in favour, but the threshold was not reached so devolution did not happen: 51.6% supported the proposal, but this was only 32.9% of the electorate given the turnout of 64%. That percentage of the electorate would rightly be considered wholly insufficient for major constitutional change.

In the nationwide 2011 referendum on proportional voting, the Act of Enablement for the referendum stipulated that the outcome of the referendum would be binding on the government.[8] This provision is unique among the referendums held to date in the UK. The level of public information and preparation for the referendum was extremely poor and the turnout low at 42%; the only regions of the UK declaring themselves in favour of proportional representation were Oxford, Cambridge, and central London – a speaking fact.

In the 2016 referendum on EU membership, as noted earlier, 37% of the electorate voted in favour of leaving; on the day this amounted to 51.89% of votes cast. The government had pledged itself *politically* to be bound by the outcome though the referendum was *officially* 'advisory only', so even though the 37% result would in any other circumstance be regarded as wholly inadequate for major constitutional change – indeed, even if the 51.89% had been *of the total electorate*, the question of legitimacy would remain – the government immediately and without due preparation plunged into the upheaval of the Brexit process.

It was a point central to this writer's argument in a previous book, *Democracy and Its Crisis* (2017), that in the tradition of representative democracy, the Westminster Parliament ought to have debated the outcome of the 2016 referendum, examining the question whether the proportion of the electorate in favour of the UK's leaving the EU was constitutionally sufficient as a recommendation to do so, not least in light of the consequences, which by the government's own lights were at best damaging to the national economy and international standing.[9] The UK Parliament did not examine and debate the outcome, and has never done so, a direct consequence of the failure of any provisions for referendums to make unequivocally clear what action must follow a referendum. Provisions for referendums are left to Parliament on a case-by-case basis and at its discretion, rather than being constitutionally defined so that differently constituted Parliaments and governments cannot make up their own version of what a referendum will be and mean. That matters should obviously be otherwise loudly makes the case for constitutional clarity as a necessity – and not just in the case of referendums.

The point about consistency is important. In the UK a trade union balloting its members on whether to take strike action has to achieve a 40% minimum of the total membership in order for a strike to be legal. In the House of Commons, a vote of 66% of the total membership is required for a dissolution of Parliament to take place outside the fixed period of five years as stipulated by the Fixed-Term Parliaments Act of 2011. The threshold for strike action, and the supermajority requirement for a dissolution of Parliament, can be explained in terms of constitutional principles. Because strike action can damage the interests of a trade union's members, the consent of a sufficient number of them is required to prevent their being prey to the actions and decisions of just a few, viz. the union's leadership. The logic of having a high supermajority bar for a dissolution of Parliament is that an election could result in a change of government, with consequent changes to the course and direction of public policy, with implications for the national interest. Both the threshold and the supermajority are accordingly there to ensure a sufficient degree of consent in light of possible consequential effects. Yet in almost all of the referendums held in the UK since 1975, no such safeguards were put in place, with the result that in the 2016 EU referendum a mere 37% of the total electorate voted for a change vastly more consequential than would standardly be effected by a general election or strike action.

This inconsistency is a mark of the readiness with which the UK's uncodified constitution can be manipulated. In effect the government of the day can choose what to treat as constitutionally acceptable. The 2016 EU referendum is rich in examples of this. To repeat the points made in the previous chapter: prior to the debate on the bill providing for the referendum – the European Referendum Bill 2015 – the House of Commons Library advised MPs that the intended referendum would be advisory only and did not bind either the government or Parliament to act on its outcome. It further pointed out that they should consider a threshold or supermajority requirement if they were minded to consider the outcome as stipulative. The then Minister for Europe followed this by explicitly assuring MPs, on the floor of the House of Commons, that there was no need for either a threshold or supermajority requirement because the referendum was only advisory.[10]

After the bill became an Act of Parliament, the Prime Minister of the day made a political pledge to treat the outcome as mandating the government to act in accordance with it (in November 2015). This contravened the assurances that the referendum was advisory only, but no redress was sought because none was possible: the government controlled the majority in the House of Commons, and the House of Commons has unlimited powers. In the event, as noted, just over a third of the electorate – 37% – voted in favour of leaving the EU. Since it was in the complete discretion of the government to treat this outcome as it wished, the post-enactment political pledge to be bound by the outcome was adhered to, and the Brexit process began.

The organizations which campaigned for leaving the EU were subsequently found to have broken the law and illegally over-spent on their campaigns. The source of some of their funding was covert and raised questions about interference in the process.[11] Despite a chorus of complaints and challenges in court, the government chose to take no action, although it was stated by a judge in the court proceedings that had the referendum not been 'advisory only' its outcome would have been voided because of the illegality.[12] One can only wonder agape at the unacceptability of this. Proper constitutional controls would have been an insurance against such a situation arising.

It is worth repeating that on the basis of the very idea of constitutionality, even if the 51.89% had been the percentage of the electorate as a whole, it would still be questionable whether it is sufficient for major constitutional change: it is nowhere near even a modest supermajority. It is also worth repeating that the debate over who should have the franchise for the referendum had resulted in exclusion of three groups of people with a material interest in the outcome: sixteen- to seventeen-year-olds, citizens who had been working or living abroad for more than fifteen years, and citizens of other EU countries working and living in the EU and paying their taxes there. (The principle of 'no taxation without representation' was not applied in this case.) As noted earlier, the 2016 EU referendum diverged in these respects from the 2014 Scottish independence referendum. This is a further example of serious inconsistency, demonstrating the impeachable lability of the UK's constitutional arrangements and the readiness with which they are manipulated for reasons of political expediency.

These two examples – respectively of the US constitution's inexpedient sclerosis and of the UK constitution's expedient unclarity and manipulability – hint at the central principles on which a democratic constitution has to be based: as follows.

The purpose of a constitution in a democracy is to lay down the way in which the purposes of democracy itself are to be met. The definition of a 'democracy', recall, is that it is an order of affairs in which the enfranchised, consisting of all the population except those too young to be expected to understand the issues at stake, set up a government and endow it with authority to act in the interests of all, doing so in a way that takes account of the range and variety of interests and preferences among the enfranchised. These are not vacuous generalizations, as preceding chapters show; they entail a definite set of constraints and prompts regarding what government in a democracy should and can be and do.

To satisfy the principles embodied in the concept of democracy a constitution must, in committing itself to them, be clear, consistent, and unambiguous. It must specify the means for resolving difficulties over its interpretation and application if such arise. It must specify how it can be modified when circumstances and sufficient agreement require. The process of adapting to circumstances has to be considered and disciplined by a due process, but it cannot be baulked or manipulated by powerful commercial interests. Constitutional change is a prime site for processes where it is genuinely a fully informed and empowered population *as a whole* that is in control, not sections or partisan interests within it.

The essential points to be addressed by a constitution concern the structure of government, its fundamental purposes and aims, the extent of its powers, how it is constituted, the rules of behaviour of those appointed to carry out its functions, the rights of all individuals within the state borders, and the remedies for violations of those rights.

Consider each of these points in more detail. A description of the structure of government concerns the *legislative* and *executive* functions and their *relationship*, the *institutions* that carry out these functions, the *personnel elected or appointed* to carry out the functions of these institutions, and the nature, extent, and limits of the *powers* both of the institutions and of the personnel elected or appointed to carry out their work.

The concept of 'how government is constituted' touches on the core matter of the enfranchised and their fundamental power of setting up and conferring authority on the institutions of government, and their periodic recall of the officers (representatives, ministers) appointed to carry out the work of those institutions.

The wording of constitutional provisions concerning the *rights* of 'all within the state's borders' signifies that it is not only citizens, but all individuals, who have fundamental rights; the enfranchised among citizens have the additional right and duty to set up and empower government by their joint authority.

Constitutional arrangements need to be made for the *judiciary*, and for the *scrutinizing bodies* charged with oversight and maintenance of standards and behaviour in the legislative and executive institutions, specifying the independence of the judiciary and the scrutinizing bodies from both these latter, and defining their own duties, powers, and the limits of their powers. Within the competence of the judiciary and the scrutinizing bodies might be powers of suspension of members of the legislature and the executive found to be in breach of the duties of their office, referring them to electors for dismissal or recall.

Changes to the constitution require a high level of consensus, but not so high that efforts at needed change, when circumstances and opinion indicate, are paralysed. Obviously there has to be a supermajority bar, because passing such a bar demonstrates an unequivocal majority in favour of the change. A bare majority is never sufficient. In many polities a two-thirds majority is regarded as the appropriate bar, but arguably this is too high; a slightly less exigent majority of 60% would be simultaneously unequivocal and attainable.

Voting should be compulsory. It is a civic duty, like paying one's taxes and binding oneself to observe the properly enacted laws of the state. Where voting is compulsory, there is automatically no need to specify a minimum threshold. Where voting is not compulsory, a minimum threshold has to be specified, because even 60% of a low turnout is insufficient to mandate constitutional change. If this percentage were required *of the electorate as a whole* then in circumstances of modest or low turnout the approving vote would have to be high, the default of not reaching that bar being the status quo. This in itself is a guarantee that constitutional change will have genuine support, and is an effective barrier to whimsy, political fashion, or misapprehensions of the kind that can arise in times of alarm in society.

These are parameters, general constraints, that leave open more detailed means by which a constitution establishes a governmental order. Local conditions and traditions might fill in the details in their own way, which is an advantage provided they conform to the entailments of the concept of democracy itself. Among the entailments are the parameters, just enumerated, that a democratic constitution must observe.

The principle at stake – and for present purposes, this is the central point – is well articulated by Tom Paine, who said that constitutions drawn up by the eighteenth-century American colonists in their several states were 'to liberty, what a grammar is to language'.[13] Elsewhere, speaking of constitutions in general, he wrote:

> A constitution is not the act of a government, but of a people constituting a government, and a government without a constitution is power without right . . . A constitution is a thing *antecedent* to a government; and a government is only the creature of a constitution . . . the continual use of the word 'constitution' in the English parliament shows there is none; and that the whole is merely a form of government without a constitution, and constituting itself with what power it pleases.[14]

He cites as a telling point the Septennial Act of 1716, in which the Parliament of Great Britain extended the duration of its own and future Parliaments' lives from three to seven years – that is, it voted itself a longer tenure of power. It had been an important feature of the post-1688 settlement that Parliaments should be re-elected every three years. 'The act by which the English parliament empowered itself to sit for seven years, shews there is no constitution in England,' Paine wrote. 'It might, by the same authority have sate any greater number of years, or for life'.[15] Thinking of the British Parliament in the first decades of the twenty-first century as one reads this, one notes, almost with incredulity, that the absolute nature of its power as thus exemplified remains unabated.

Of course, the British constitution has continued variously to evolve, change, and grow in other respects over time, providing defenders of its uncodified status with the comfortable argument that it is flexible and adaptable, responsive to circumstance. In truth, it is a ramshackle affair, a patchwork of expediency and accident, whose 'flexibilities' occur in response to historically parochial needs and urgencies which then stick anachronistically in the state's practices of governance thereafter. It is, in short, an amateur affair, which is made up as it goes along, and which is conveniently adaptable for whoever holds the reins of power at a given time. Definition of the purposes, duties and powers (and their limits) of the organs and officers of state would prevent the subordination of the state's affairs to mere party-political machination; sensible provision for achieving maximally consensual and timely changes to the constitution in response to changing conditions is not beyond the intelligence of humankind. How to adapt a constitution when necessary is a *practical* question; the supposed difficulty of making suitable changes is not an argument against the *principle* that the constitution should be clear, consistent, and understandable by all so that the institutions of state and those who operate them can be held accountable.

One of the most significant points of all concerns the system of representation. It is clear from the foregoing that the principles of democracy entail that it must be a constitutional requirement that an electoral system be such as genuinely to reflect the diversity of preferences among the enfranchised, subject to protection against minoritarian super-influence on the government process. The argument for this merits emphasizing again, from a fresh direction, as follows.

The existing UK and US constitutions are examples of arrangements aimed at retaining power in the hands of those who populate the institutions of government, because they always hand control to one or other party in a two-party system. The word 'control' is used advisedly; these constitutional arrangements impose a series of filters on the diverse expressions of preference and interest in the populace, apparently to siphon from them rational and orderly government which fulfils the purposes of government 'sufficiently', this being the point of the idea of 'representation' in a representative democracy. But in fact an electoral system that produces a two-party political oligopoly exists as much, if not more, to ensure that those who capture the institutions of government are able to operate them to effect in the service of their partisan policy objectives. On the one hand it might seem reasonable that this should be so, because constant interference from the Babel of interests in the populace – their pushing and pulling at the governmental process, with the strongest or best-funded interests out-muscling others who have legitimate claims but smaller purses – would hamper effective government. But the actual effect is that when the levers of power are captured by a partisan group, a faction, a political party, with an agenda that serves its own sectional interests above others, the inclusive purposes of government are not best served. And this regularly happens in FPTP systems where the powers of government are endowed by a constitution that itself does not scrupulously reflect the principles of democracy.

Matters are far worse if the faction in question is elected on an absolute minority of the vote, as almost invariably happens in FPTP systems. But wherever the political order consists in a single party forming the government, the familiar risks and realities of partisanship result.

A good system of proportional representation – by this meaning one that reflects the diversity among the electorate but does not allow minoritarian super-influence – can and most often does reduce the degree of factional control of government. This is because the formation of coalitions drains some degree – sometimes a considerable degree – of the politics from practical government once agreement is reached, largely restricting the *political* dimension to elections and negotiations over coalition arrangements. Once in government on the basis of agreement, coalition partners restrain each other; in this lies the principal virtue of electoral systems that produce governments of agreement. Only political activists will disagree that this embodiment of the principle that *government should transcend politics* is a good thing.

Best of all is a system where the executive and the legislature are fully independent of each other, the former answerable to the latter, and each able to initiate legislation and action, with mechanisms for mutual constraining – these involving a revising second chamber and an independent judiciary. This is the fundamental Montesquieu-version of the 1688 model but with full enfranchisement and proportional voting attached, the latter applying both to the principal legislative chamber and to the separate executive office.

A constitution that occupies the space within the constraints just described will be a democratic constitution. Consider what this would imply for the US. It would not permit a situation in

130

which the states of California and Wyoming each send two senators to Washington although California has seventy times the
population of Wyoming. Because small states other than those
on the eastern seaboard tend to be 'red' states, the Senate has a
permanent conservative bias that does not reflect sentiment or
need in the US overall. It also means that small states get a
proportionately larger share than populous ones of distributed
national resources. It has been pointed out that if the senators
from the twenty-six least populated states always voted together,
they would control the Senate despite representing just 17% of
the US population. When the Connecticut Compromise of
1787 was adopted on how the Senate would be constituted,
there was no way to foresee how the population of the US would
grow and be distributed. The urgent need is for more Senate
seats elected proportionally to population.

A constitution respecting the principles of democracy would
outlaw gerrymandering – manipulation of electoral district
boundaries – which is a persistent problem in the US, and results
in the majority of congressional districts never changing hands
in elections. Such a constitution would make salutary changes in
further key respects. The Electoral College is a desperate anomaly, twice in the two decades before these words were written
handing the Presidency to individuals who secured a minority
of the popular vote. The method for impeaching a President is
cumbersome, favouring the possessor of the White House
however incompetent or unsuitable for office. Treating the existing constitution as if it were holy writ makes reform difficult,
sometimes to the point of impossibility – a serious deficit. The
balance of powers between the legislature and the executive,
although their separation is in itself a good and important
feature, requires adjustment: one crucial example is that the
House of Representatives, as the directly elected house (*pace*

the FPTP voting system), has difficulty stopping a war if a President wishes to continue it; and so on other major foreign policy matters. In short, as so many US writers on their constitution argue, the existing constitution is outdated and in parts significantly ambiguous, and requires refreshment.[16]

But it is at least a constitution, and a healthy sense of the importance of a constitution as defining the nature and extent of governmental powers, and entrenching fundamental rights, is widespread among thinking Americans. In the UK the deliberate adherence to a confused, confusing, befogged set of conventions and traditions, intermingled with a patchwork of statutes and ambiguously festooned with revocable sequestrations of powers to devolved authorities and treaty partners such as European Union states, continues to serve the interests of governments drawn from one or other of the two political parties whose oligopoly is preserved by an undemocratic electoral system, governments which in their control of the legislature have unlimited powers to do what they like. I repeat that Sir Leslie Stephen's remark in his book *The Science of Ethics* (1882) that if Parliament 'decided that all blue-eyed babies should be murdered the preservation of blue-eyed babies would be illegal' is as true today as it was when he wrote it. He added that 'legislators must go mad before they could pass such a law, and subjects be idiotic before they could submit to it', but he lived before the 1930s in Germany, and therefore spoke too soon. Uninhibited by a clear constitution, today's British Parliament could enact just such a law. The Levitsky–Ziblatt–Mill (now add Stephen) belief in self-restraint, in 'constitutional morality', is an extremely poor alternative to codification of the arrangements defining the institutions and governing the behaviour of the holders – always temporary, remember – of legislative and executive office.

What of judiciaries? The independence of judges from

politics and government is enormously important, and has led to a norm of tenure – of lifelong and unremovable office (except for misconduct) – for judges once appointed. But unrestricted tenure for judges is undesirable: appointments should be for a stated period, even if the period is long. There tends to be a direct relationship between disillusionment and conservatism with increasing age, and it is a generous interpretation of human capacity to see how a justice in his eighties at this time of writing, most of whose life has been lived without the internet, and without the advanced technologies of miniaturized and powerful communications now available and providing a multiplicity of social media platforms, can fully appreciate how things seem from the point of view of anyone less than half his age – which is to say: by far most of the world's population.

The appointment process to senior judicial posts is highly political in the US, which is a great fault. Whatever system of appointment is instituted, it has to be immunized against political partisanship. If judges are to determine the constitutionality of acts of government, the government cannot appoint those who are to sit in judgment of their acts, or the acts of their opponents: the point is perfectly simple. In the UK there has long been criticism of the fact that the higher reaches of the judiciary are very largely composed of white men who were educated at private schools and Oxbridge. In a diverse and pluralistic age the significant institutions of state and society should reflect the realities. It is not as if the high quality of mind and thought expected of those charged with high responsibilities are to be found only in that small percentage of the population who went to private school.

6

RIGHTS IN A DEMOCRACY

In the seventeenth century the idea that people have certain 'natural rights' which are inalienable – meaning that they cannot be overridden or taken away by anyone or anything – formed an essential part of the idea that the state comes into being through a contract between people who, in the 'state of nature', cannot enjoy their natural rights in safety.[1] In John Locke's version of contractarian theory, the fundamental rights are those to life, personal liberty, and secure possession of one's property. By the end of the eighteenth century the idea of *natural* rights – rights possessed by everyone just in virtue of existing as a human being – had come under attack. Jeremy Bentham called them 'nonsense on stilts', and Edmund Burke criticized them as mere abstractions, arguing instead that the source of rights is tradition and inherited institutions and practices, and that overturning them – as in the French Revolution, against which he inveighed – would result in anarchy.

Bentham wrote a critique – called *Anarchical Fallacies* – of the French Revolution's declaration of the 'natural, inalienable and sacred . . . Rights of Man and the Citizen' (1789), arguing that 'Right . . . is the child of law: from real laws come real rights: but from laws of nature, fancied and invented by poets, rhetoricians, and dealers in moral and intellectual poisons come imaginary rights, a bastard brood of monsters, gorgons and chimeras dire.'[2] Burke denied the universality of rights by arguing that the rights won through historical struggle meant that different states – for example, England and France – had developed different regimes of rights suited to their own character as nations. Both Bentham and Burke were opposed to their contemporary Tom Paine who eloquently championed the idea of natural rights, arguing that 'civil rights' derive from them and provide them with their justification.[3]

Both Bentham and Burke took the view that rights exist only in society, and cannot exist outside or before society, and that they come into existence as a result of law or agreement; which means that rights are conferred, not automatically or intrinsically possessed. For those who think as Locke does, rights are understood *negatively*, that is, as protecting against interference, obstruction, or depredation. Nothing else is required for the protection of one's own rights than that others do not interfere or obstruct one's exercise of them. Others are not required positively to do or provide anything; they have only to refrain. The idea that rights are *positively* conferred by law or agreement is consistent with the ideas of both negative and positive rights. A negative right is a liberty; a positive right is an entitlement. Both place obligations on others, either to refrain from interfering or obstructing, or to provide what a positive right entitles its bearer to have. But it is easy to see that the obligations imposed by positive rights are more onerous.

On what grounds did the member states of the United Nations adopt the Universal Declaration of Human Rights in 1948? The Declaration itself claims that rights flow from 'the inherent dignity of the human person'. Critics point out that the concept of 'human dignity' presupposes a particular set of moral

views about persons and about what conduces to human flourishing – or at least, must do so if the notion of 'dignity' is to be
less vague. Which view should we adopt, critics ask, given the
marked differences among such views in different traditions of
thought and culture? This is in effect a relativist version of scepticism about the idea that rights inhere in us purely in virtue of
our being human.

Context provides the answer to this scepticism. The
Declaration of Human Rights was written and adopted in the
immediate aftermath of horrendous episodes of inhumane
behaviour in the war years immediately preceding. That context
dramatizes the truth that the roots of rights lie in the experience
of wrongs. The cruelty, injustice, prejudice, and wanton disre-
gard for human individuality that produced such an immense
amount of suffering in those years were more eloquent than two
thousand years of philosophical reflection on the justification
for insisting that each human individual has a right to life, to
liberty, to privacy, to protection from inhumane treatment, and
more.

There are different ways of unpacking this point. Irrespective
of culture and history, there are certain fundamentals about
human beings that must give us pause in considering how they
should be treated – note 'must'. Very few sentient beings like to
be hungry, in pain, cold, lonely, afraid, and confined against their
will or inclination.[4] Human beings further dislike injustices,
when they are aware of them, such as being discriminated
against, barred from significant opportunities, and denied a fair
share of distributions. Most of us do not want others to impose
these experiences or conditions on us. These facts tell us much
about what we are to think of values. To speak in this way, especially about the dislike of hunger, pain, cold, and fear, is to disagree straight away with the 'is–ought' proscription against

136

seeing moral obligations in natural facts. For awareness of these natural facts is inscribed in us as social beings, and they are fundamental to judgments about what has political and moral value and disvalue. It has taken a long time for the injustices of discrimination and exclusion to be contested, because for most of that long time they were claimed (by those in control of the discourse) not to be injustices – for example, by the alleged inferiority in physical and intellectual power of women, or the alleged cultural primitiveness of non-white people, or the alleged innate superiority of aristocrats to peasants, and so on. These *devaluations* were themselves predicated on a rejection of the fact–value divide, illustrating not only the interrelationship of fact and value but also how important it is to get the *facts* right in determining values.

Personal experience, social sympathies, and history together inform us about the value-relevant facts. On that basis rights can be identified that individuals must be regarded as having so that they can live self-determining lives and have the chance, if they take it, to flourish.[5] Rights open the space within which that is possible. We need neither the mythology of a state of nature, nor the imprimatur of positive law, to provide the ground for rights: personal experience, social sympathies, and history together license *laying claim* to rights, which the intelligence of our species sees with equal quickness and clarity to make good mutual as well as individual sense. One could call this an *arrogatory theory of rights*, given that we arrogate rights to ourselves and on behalf of our fellows, on the basis of our understanding of what, on our best sympathetic understanding of the human condition, is valuable and what is not.

In saying above that each human individual has a right to life, to liberty, to privacy, to protection from inhumane treatment, 'and more', it is this 'more' which is of particular interest to democratic theory. The question to be asked is: What does the concept of *democracy* – the concept of the fundamental authority of the people in a state and society, their participation and inclusion in both, and their equality in respect of citizenship – entail in the way of the entitlements and expectations of each individually, and the reciprocal obligations of each to each? The intention of the standard set of rights, as just noted, is to open a space around individuals to protect them and offer them ways forward, if they apply their energies; but having the door left open is not enough if you cannot walk. The concept of democracy therefore implies something further in the way of *enabling* participation – for participation in a democracy is not merely a matter of voting, but of sharing in what the joint endeavour of the society, as captured in the purposes of government, can deliver, given that government is constituted precisely to deliver those outcomes for *all*.

It was this kind of thinking that prompted the adoption by the UN of covenants of civil, political, and economic rights as a more detailed and more committal description of what should be the case for good human lives to be possible. Whereas the Covenant on Civil and Political Rights largely iterates and expands upon the basic rights of the 1948 Declaration, the Covenant on Economic, Social and Cultural Rights goes much further. Rights to life, liberty, privacy, freedom of conscience, and protection from inhumane treatment, are obvious. But rights to work, social security, health, free education, and 'participation in cultural life', seem to some critics to go too far *as rights*. At most, such critics might say, they are desiderata, but it is for the individual to achieve them, if she wishes to and can; it is not for society to provide them.

It is, however, these very desiderata that the concept of democracy challenges us to consider. Let it be recalled that

138

rights in a democracy are those entailed by the idea that a democracy is *for the people*. Spelling out what that means takes us directly to such ideas as: the right not to be defrauded of opportunity; the right to be protected against exploitation by a system, by other individuals or corporations; the right not to be trampled underfoot in situations where inequality of gifts, even in circumstance of equality of opportunity (if they could be made to prevail), will inevitably result in inequality of outcomes. And both individuals and the corporate being of society itself have always therefore to reckon with the destructive nature of social and economic inequality.

This point merits expansion. All societies and economies are in perpetual transition, everywhere and in all periods of history. People at the front end of change stand to benefit most; people in the rear typically lag behind and suffer – those in the rust-belt industries made obsolete by new technologies, the older workers unable to retrain and adapt, the communities bypassed in the rush to a different future. There is a clear justification for a safety net and for positive action to improve the circumstances of those at the rear of change. A familiar neoliberal argument is that these very inequalities are in fact drivers of economic progress: the people at the front wish to maintain their position, the people at the back push to catch up, the joint outcome of these impulses is advance. But this view ignores the built-in disadvantages and barriers of the social and economic order – at any point there are people who start way ahead in the race, and others way behind, making for a huge wastage of human possibility in the deep and persistent inequalities thus represented. In the inclusivity implied in the concept of democracy, each and all have a claim to appropriate consideration in light of this pervasive fact.

The putatively robust vision of an economic order full of striving pushers and pullers, between them rolling forward the wagon of progress, overlooks the grave downside of economic libertarianism, which has been known – too often – to be a licence to exploit and defraud, so that there is sometimes a paper-thin divide between business and (not to dress up the point) organized crime – an object lesson is provided by the railroad companies in nineteenth-century North America, but other examples are legion.[6]

Consider the argument between neoclassical and Keynesian macroeconomic theorists. The former believe that markets will clear themselves – adjust toward equilibrium – through the price mechanism, and that destabilization of markets occurs when governments interfere. In a utopian version of this view, full employment will be maintained because in business cycle downturns wages will fall to keep workers employed. Likewise, interest rates will always reflect the balance between savings and investment, falling when savings are high and rising when they are low relative to investment needs; and the balance of cross-border trade will move toward equilibrium through adjustments in exchange rates. And so on. Keynesians point out that markets are not the frictionless mechanisms thus assumed by neoclassical theorists: price 'stickiness', gaming of the markets, and irrational sentiment among market players are permanently destabilizing factors. The empirical evidence supports this. That markets can rise and fall excessively is shown by the periodic crashes such as 1929 and 2008 (and a number between) – together with the facts that unemployment rises when economic activity slows, that interest rates do not fall as fast as savings increase, and the like. In the decade following the crash of 2008 the UK governments of 2010 and 2015 applied austerity measures to reduce government debt, in repudiation of the Keynesian logic that governments should borrow and spend in a downturn, and save and repay in an upturn. The social effect was catastrophic, involving dramatic cuts in health, education, policing, housing, and welfare spending. The taproots of the Brexit phenomenon lie in domestic economic policy not, as many 'Leave' voters had been persuaded, in anything to do with the EU, membership of which had if anything been a buffer against even worse austerity effects.

The salient point in these thoughts is that, according to neoclassical theory, the 'labour market' is one of the moving parts in the adjustment mechanism along with the product, service and financial markets, employment and earnings varying in accordance with the rise and fall of demand in the other markets. This is to treat living human beings, with families and concerns additional to their role as employees, as mere units of account. In a democratic political order in which the interests and welfare of all constitute a chief purpose of government formed on the authority of almost all of the 'all' – namely, the enfranchised – this is morally unacceptable; and legislation in most advanced economies on workers' rights reflects the fact that even when profit – the relentless pursuit of which is a highly distorting factor in markets, to the detriment chiefly of the labour market – remains more important than human beings, the consciences of such polities cannot accept the full implication of the neoclassical view.

The cost of 'workers' rights' may well be lower profits and a lower GDP, though there are theorists who point out that gains in productivity resulting from a happier and more committed workforce offset the costs, at least to some extent. But profits and GDP are not the only, or perhaps even the right, metrics for measuring the quality of a state and the society forming it. Perhaps high profits and an ever-growing GDP are signs not of health but of exploitation of people, together with increased risks to social stability and increased risks to the environment. Perhaps one of the outcomes of a relentless pursuit of profit and economic growth is eventually the reaction of populism and discontent in society, and disturbance of the tranquillity of the state.

'The right to participate' in a democracy is not, as has been iterated several times in the foregoing, restricted to the right to vote. It is a right to inclusion; a right, at the very least, to the absence of barriers to participation – but as this is in practice not enough by itself, it entails a right to *enablement* to participation. This is already recognized in the social provision of education and health services, given that possession of a significant minimum of both are indispensable prerequisites for people to participate. But is this yet enough? Unless the education and the health service are good, it will not be. Struggling, overworked, understaffed, and underfunded schools and clinics, even if provided free at the point of use to the entire population, will not achieve that enablement well enough or often enough. Consider schools: in the state sector, despite the remarkable dedication and endeavours of teachers – for teaching is a vocation, and few with no vocation for it survive in it long – the number of young people who are placed, in the outcome, on the same footing as those who have been at the best (mainly private) schools even only as regards attainment, leaving aside all other predisposing advantages, is by a great margin far too small. Bored and uninterested school pupils are so because classes are too big, teachers are too stretched, and too little time is devoted to pupils as individuals. In a society in which amounts of money are supposed to constitute the measure of personal value, people in relatively low-paying professions such as teaching are not regarded as role models and stars.

Conservatives like Edmund Burke, and many after him into the present, observe that institutions emerge from practice and tradition which are themselves the product of compromises in response to needs; and they add the claim that this – the fact of their organic growth over time, hallowed by use and age – is what constitutes their worth. This evolutionary picture is typically framed by more recent theorists such as Friedrich Hayek on analogy with biological evolution, as having no designing mind at work in them, but instead as emerging organically from historical and social processes through the pressures of need and circumstance. Adam Smith and Burke are quoted in support of this view, and with them Adam Ferguson: 'Nations stumble upon establishments, which are indeed the result of human action but not the result of human design.'[7]

There are two things wrong with this picture. The first is that organic growth and age are not by themselves guarantees of worth or, even if the compromises were effective in their day, of continued fitness for purpose. The second is that it is nonsense to suppose that no designing mind was involved; of course there were minds involved at the point of creation of the compromises. When these compromises themselves become compromising, designing minds get to work to reform or overthrow them; the principal driver of political change is the way old forms and practices, like shoes outgrown, begin to pinch. Those served by a given structure fight to retain it; those in need of new structures fight to tear the old one down, whether or not their utopian vision of a bright new structure is realized – which of course they hope it will be – or whether the process of a new organic growth of compromises results. More usually it is the latter, especially after revolutions, whose outcomes are rarely inherited by those who start them.

But instead of leaving the organization of the state and society to chance, to the accidental emergence of genius or cunning in an individual here and another individual there, and to the wavering fortunes of political factions, the rights entailed by the very concept of democracy require something more definite: in short, they require clear statement and transparent application and defence. Alternatively put, democratic rights require codification in a constitution designed to serve all in the *demos*, and capable of sensible, mature-minded adaptation to changing circumstances.

It is worth repeating at this juncture the important insight, first offered in chapter 1, that every nation is a congeries of individuals and minorities. The emergence of a majority view on a particular issue is a phenomenon composed of the overlapping Venn diagrams of a sufficient number of minorities. But everyone is in a minority of some kind on some question. And everyone is an individual. This is why the idea of rights is so important: everyone's individual and minority status requires defence against such majorities as emerge from time to time – on capital punishment, disapproval of homosexuality, opposition to abortion, hostility to immigration, or whatever else arises to preoccupy the public mind, at times because real questions of principle have to be confronted, at times inflamed by tabloid-press attitudes pushing a partisan agenda or seeking profits.

Democracy is about bringing the individuals and minorities of a state and society together in relationships that command agreement and cooperation for what that can produce in the way of benefits for all – *for all*: not just the majority, and certainly not just the most powerful and effective minority. The balance of 'all' and 'each' in this connection is chiefly a matter of *politics*, but the limits beyond which politics can take the balance off the horizontal is a matter of a larger framework agreement – the constitutional provisions that prevent harm to individuals or the squeezing of any minorities in the putative interests of other minorities or of the other minorities collected, for a given purpose at a particular time, as a majority.

The totality of the enfranchised is 'the constituent power' in the state and society. It is so whether or not it acts as a totality, or through a majority constituted by a sufficient coalition of minorities. But it has to be a defined power, and limited in a number of directions to protect minorities and individuals – limited by the boundaries set by rights, clearly stated and transparently enforced. The rights guaranteed by a constitution, like the law, must apply to everyone equally, be justified, and be certain: when Locke spoke of 'security' he did not mean (or only mean) the kind that results from an honest and dedicated police force protecting society against menace; he also meant assurance of one's rights and knowing that the laws will not be misapplied or suddenly and arbitrarily change. But the idea of the equal applicability of the law is, although sufficient for legal justice, not by itself enough for social justice, as demonstrated by Anatole France's praise for 'the majestic equality of the law, which prohibits both rich and poor from sleeping under bridges, begging in the streets, and stealing bread.'[8] For this, the addition of democratic rights is essential.

In the US, conceptions of individual rights sit at an odd angle to the congratulatory self-image of the state as a democracy. The great American anomaly is that the *demos* in the US is instinctively libertarian and against power, against government, despite the latter being constituted by democratic acts of the majority. America says repeatedly that it is a democracy, that it believes in democracy and champions it – even goes to war to protect it or establish it in places far from home – yet it is actually highly minoritarian in its attitude to state and especially federal power. One might almost say that Americans believe in 'the will of the minority of one, viz. me' (for any 'me'), and this not just in the hinterlands of mid-western states. Hamilton in the *Federalist Papers* cleverly employed this sentiment against itself, standing it on its head by using the ingrained suspicion of government – a suspicion there from the very outset of the colonies, populated by people who had fled the tyranny of monarchs and ecclesiastical establishments in Europe – to dilute the concept of popular sovereignty with the need for what are in effect aristocratic institutions of Senate and judiciary and the monarchical institution of a Presidency. But it is well that Hamilton failed in another endeavour, namely, his opposition to a Bill of Rights, because it is this aspect of the US Constitution which, in embodying and buttressing the underlying political sentiment just identified, maintains the legitimacy of the democratic ideal by keeping any potential tyranny of a majority off the backs of minorities, including the minority of one. In this respect the US is an exemplar of the importance of both constitutionality and the entrenchment of rights, despite the ossifications it suffers in both respects to its own harm. For democracy is about rights, the rights to selfhood, participation, and inclusion as the fundamental justification for the whole range of rights valued in societies that aspire to be called democratic.

7

THE SUBVERSION
OF DEMOCRACY

A military coup is one obvious way to subvert democracy. But the way it is in fact subverted in what we take to be the world's leading democracies today is more insidious though no less visible, and although just one of the following factors by itself damages and can even derail democracy, combinations of them make the problem greatly worse. A survey of the world's Westminster Model democracies, standard or adapted, will show that none of them has fewer than five of the following six democracy-undermining factors present in them: my challenge to any critic is to prove otherwise. I itemize the factors in no particular order.

The degree to which individual citizens feel that they have little or no influence over the processes of politics and government is exacerbated by electoral systems which are unrepresentative. FPTP systems notoriously disenfranchise all who vote for losing candidates, and typically yield majorities in legislatures on minorities of the popular vote. The feeling that one's vote is not going to make a difference inclines one not to vote. The more a voter feels alienated from the system, the yet more alienated she becomes. FPTP systems hand government to a party, a faction, rather than – as proportional systems do – obliging parties to come together to form governments based on a wider franchise serving a wider range of interests.[1] Partisan policies favour certain sections of society against others; their tendency is to increase divisions, inequalities, and social tensions.

Citizens can be alienated from the processes of politics and government even in proportionally representative systems if politicians are more interested in their careers than in serving the public interest, with politics itself a playground of professional politicians whose interest in working the system for career ends is constrained only by re-electability considerations, which is when citizens are noticed. In every Westminster Model democracy politics is a professional career for almost all who become involved as representatives, party functionaries, and advisors. Together these factors place a rampart between politics and government on the one hand, and citizens on the other, creating and perpetuating the alienation at issue. When citizens do not feel that they are making a difference or being heard, they switch off – which is convenient for the political establishment itself – or in certain circumstances, when frustration has reached a pitch, they make drastic choices, voting for *outré* candidates or parties usually on the more extreme wings of the political spectrum, in order to give the political establishment a kicking. The results of this are not guaranteed to be productive: the two words 'Trump' and 'Brexit' illustrate why.

The toxic effects of political careerism are intensified by systems of party discipline which make representatives serve the party's interest – in order thereby to serve their own personal interest – rather than what their judgment and conscience might tell them is the national interest. This is the norm, not the exception, in Westminster Model Parliaments. The exercise of control over MPs by parliamentary whips is taken for granted; a party votes to order as a bloc, and in all but exceptional circumstances failure to obey that order can result in expulsion ('withdrawal of the whip') which means no party endorsement and support at the subsequent election – hence, loss of job – or at least a blight on the individual's record, lessening her chances of advancement and office. To exercise this degree of control over representatives the whips use persuasion, promises, and too often underhand methods – for just one but very speaking example, a Conservative MP in the British Parliament in 2019 revealed that several of his former army colleagues had been approached covertly by his party's whips seeking information that could, if made public, be an embarrassment to him, or worse. The MP in question, Johnny Mercer, used his Twitter account to announce this, commenting on a warning he had received from an army colleague that the whips were in search of 'dirt': 'Third one of these I've had of late, from an old Army contact. Contrast the values and ethos of that institution vs Parliament, and you'll start to find answers of how we got the UK politically into such a mess. Values, integrity, ethos – never been more important, or more scarce.'[2]

Accordingly, even if the electoral system is reasonably proportional, political careerism, and what it makes possible in the form of party control, undermines democracy. Couple a FPTP system with party-dominated Parliaments, and you have a deeply undermined democracy. There might be a multiplicity of parties, with secret ballots and freedom of speech and the press – the features standardly invoked as descriptors of democracy – but these are not enough to constitute democracy by themselves, especially if what they produce is government by party machine.

Matters are worse in Westminster Model systems even than this, however, because of the absence of a separation of powers between the executive and the legislature. This is *the* cardinal failing of the model, and the egregious example of Brexit in the UK illustrates just how fragile and vulnerable the model is to certain kinds of predictable stress.

Consider a party which has a majority in the legislature, and from which therefore the executive is drawn. If the leadership of that party is captured by one of its internal groupings on an outer wing of the political spectrum, this wing controls the government and the country, and can implement its preferred policies whether or not there is majority support for them in the country – and indeed, as we see, usually on the basis of minority support only. The executive is in an entrenched position from which great effort is needed to expel it, even if these policies are extremely divisive and contested, so long as it controls the legislative majority and the business order of Parliament.

This is the situation that obtained in the Brexit debacle in the UK following the 2016 EU membership referendum (see chapter 5). Recall the following: that Brexit was a policy of the political right wing; that in the 2016 referendum it secured only 37% of the total electorate in favour, but implemented the policy nevertheless; that by the European Parliament elections in 2019 this support had dropped below 17% of the electorate, but although the leader of the governing party resigned, the party itself did not change policy.[3] By some three years into the Brexit process the executive's control of the legislature, already compromised by having to form an arrangement with a small far-right Northern Ireland party to keep it in government as a result of losing its majority in the 2017 general election, had been sufficiently weakened for it to lose some highly significant votes in the House of Commons, though it continued to win confidence motions because a majority of MPs did not wish to trigger another general election. Earlier in the process some serious missteps – for a major example, the triggering of the Article 50 process for the UK to leave the EU, but without any impact assessments, plans, or preparations in place – had been taken because the executive still had control of the legislative majority, and the missteps could not be defeated on the floor of Parliament.

In 2017 the government of Theresa May attempted to circumvent Parliament in its triggering of the Article 50 process for taking the UK out of the European Union, by use of the executive's 'prerogative powers', these formerly being the powers exercisable by the monarch independently of Parliament. The English Civil War of 1642–51 and the 'Glorious Revolution' of 1688 between them initiated a transfer of these powers from monarch to Parliament. The government of Boris Johnson again sought to circumvent Parliament in 2019 by proroguing it – that is, shutting it down for a period – so that MPs opposed to the UK's leaving the EU without a negotiated deal (or at all) could not oppose a 'No Deal' exit. Both these endeavours, each highly questionable in terms of constitutional principle, turned in significant part upon the absence of a separation of powers between executive and legislature.

So: without a separation of powers the executive controls the legislature; whichever group in the ruling party controls the executive therefore controls everything. Government is by faction. So long as the faction in question is pragmatic and reasonably moderate, no one will notice. But if the faction that gains control is situated at an extremity of the political spectrum, the result will be destabilizing, divisive, and chaos-engendering, exactly the Brexit situation.

Could such a situation arise where the executive and legislative powers are exercised in separate institutions? Yes, if the following series of conditions simultaneously obtain: if one of the parties represented in the legislature has a majority over all the others combined, if strong party discipline is imposed upon it, if the majority can control the business of the legislature (rather than the legislature observing an independently fixed order of business that cannot be manipulated to the advantage of any one grouping), and if the executive is fully aligned with that majority so that each does the other's behest – then yes, such a situation could arise, for it would precisely mimic the current Westminster Model arrangements. Given that this is so, it would be the point of constitutional requirements on the relationship between the legislature and the executive that the sequence of hypotheticals just set out is rendered unlikely to obtain. Indeed, it could quite easily be constitutionally prevented as a norm by a proportionally representative electoral system for the legislature. If the legislature is composed of a number of parties none of which has a majority over all the others combined, and if the chief executive is elected separately and appoints her own administration from outside the legislature, the desideratum of the legislature being in control of the executive, and not the other way around, would be achieved.

If an institutional separation of powers does not exist, then a proportional electoral system which standardly produces coalition government is the next best means of ensuring that the levers of governmental power are not captured by a clique which can, with relative impunity, manipulate them according to its partisan agenda.

In a situation where an executive proposing to act in a certain way has to secure the approval of a legislature independent of it, with a fixed set of requirements to do so – at the minimum presenting the rationale, the evidence in favour, and evaluations of the consequences and effects – something like the Article 50 trigger in the Brexit experience would have been highly unlikely if not indeed impossible. The point is that there is a far better chance of more considered and rational government – government not almost always sailing before the winds of factional politics and ideology – where the executive and legislative powers are separate, than if they are the same as in the Westminster Model. The margin for error, and particularly catastrophic error, is considerably less.

As the UK's experience in the Brexit crisis illustrates, the fundamental flaws of the Westminster Model make it highly vulnerable to producing poor government under stress, and poor management of difficult situations. This has been shown repeatedly if one looks at cases, in which the UK itself is alas very rich: Suez in 1956, the disastrous 1970s, Brexit.[4] British government during the Second World War was a coalition government working in the national rather than partisan interest, under a discipline imposed by dangerous external events. That same discipline – joint endeavour in the national interest – is what the principles of democracy say should be imposed on government always and everywhere, whether in peace or war. But the Westminster Model governance structure does not deliver that. It is risky, for under pressure it is too likely to foster and exacerbate problems.

Between 2010 and the EU referendum of 2016 the austerity policies of the UK's Conservative-led government widened inequality and led to a rise in poverty levels, an increase in the use of food banks, the reduction of welfare support, and cuts in policing, education, and health services. The result was disaffection, and the predictable swing to radical alternatives in polling booths. Social solidarity and the provision of good public services are key to a stable and flourishing society, however much the flourishing of private enterprise matters also (for, after

all, it provides the tax base for the former). The austerity measures were a party-political platform commitment. How the fall-
out from the 2008 international financial crash might have been
handled differently is a matter for speculation; in circumstances
where the party that controlled the finance ministry (in the UK
called the 'Exchequer') had its party commitments on the
matter, and could put them into effect because they controlled
the legislature, arguments about better alternatives went
unheeded.[5]

In the US the separation of powers failure arises in the subordination of the judicial system to the political process. All
Supreme Court and Appeals Court justices are political appointees, and their long tenure of office means that the political
complexion of the courts has a major effect on American society. At time of writing several states have introduced restrictions
on abortion, seeking to have the *Roe v. Wade* decision of 1973
tested in a Supreme Court which, as a result of the Trump
Presidency, has swung to the right, and is therefore likely to
overturn that landmark decision which has had such a positive
impact on women's lives, health, and choices. This is indeed a
test case for whether justice should be allowed to be so much a
matter for political influence. It cannot be beyond the wit of
humankind to devise ways of populating judicial benches with
excellence in legal expertise but which more accurately reflect
the diversity in society, and are based on a broader consensus in
society than is typical of party-political interests.

Both the foregoing points raise questions about whether
there is fitness for purpose in the *constitutional* arrangements for
the institutions of government and their interrelationships. If
the constitution is too vague, lacking clarity and being too open
to manipulative interpretations (the UK situation), or too inflex-
ible and in parts outdated (the US situation), the question of

how to strike an appropriate balance of powers will be more difficult to answer, as problems arising either from lack of separation between powers, or mutual obstruction arising from conflicts between the powers, will be more difficult to resolve. The desideratum here is for clear and transparent constitutional arrangements that are themselves capable of evolution in an orderly and careful way when appropriate. Both the UK and the US are dramatically in need of reform in this respect.

Then there is the question of *money*. The US is described as a plutocracy, and not just because the enormous sums spent on elections to Congress and the White House imply that money is the premise of politics and thereby of government. The very structure of American society is designed – some say warped – by the presence of money in the political system. In his *Plutocracy in America* (2019) Ronald Formisano argues that the US has two tax systems, one for wealthy individuals and corporations, and one for everyone else. The immiseration of people at the lower end of the income scale is itself a commercial opportunity for loan sharks – payday loans, auto title loans, 'tax preparation' centres that claim to secure refunds: Formisano calculates that $30 billion are extracted annually from the poorest in society by such means. 'Inequality is a disease pumped into the system' by the infrastructure of the economy itself, an infrastructure created by political choices influenced by those most capable of purchasing their implementation.[6]

In *The Good Society* (1996) J. K. Galbraith observed that the political dialectic had, by the time he wrote that book, changed from one between capital and labour to one between rich and poor, and he warned of the dangers of increasing inequality between them – warnings which, unheeded, have proved all too well founded. The political dialectic between rich and poor is, he wrote:

an unequal contest; the rich and comfortable have influence and money. And they vote. The concerned and the poor have numbers, but many of the poor, alas, do not vote. There is democracy, but in no slight measure it is a democracy of the fortunate. A defining issue between these two groupings, as is well recognized, is the role of government. For the poor, the government can be central to their well-being, and for some even to survival. For the rich and comfortable, it is a burden save when, as in the case of military expenditure, Social Security and the rescue of failed financial institutions, it serves their particular interest. Then it ceases to be a burden and becomes a social necessity, a social good, as certainly it is not when the government serves the poor.[7]

A plutocracy is a state in which the rich rule. On the foregoing evidence, it is evident that in the US matters are skewed considerably in favour of the better-off, and the argument is that this is because the better-off, and especially the rich, profoundly influence government through the access that donations give them. It costs more than a million dollars to run for a seat in the House of Representatives, about ten million dollars to run for a seat in the Senate, and the average spend in the last couple of decades by the candidates left standing in presidential races is well over $500 million each. Money in politics comes from three sources: donations to individual candidates and political parties, federal funding, and 'superPACs' (PAC means 'political action committee') allegedly not supporting particular individuals or parties but 'political causes'. The two former technically have limits imposed by electoral law; superPAC spending is unlimited. Needless to say, legal decisions allowing superPAC activity (the Supreme Court in *Citizens United v. FEC* and the D. C. Circuit Court of Appeals in *SpeechNOW.org v. FEC*)[8] were highly controversial. As an example of the Constitution's sanctified standing, the First Amendment free speech right is invoked in defence of the right to apply unlimited funds to your chosen political cause – a polemicist might say: the right to buy the government.

An argument that has increasingly gained the status of orthodoxy is that the relationship between money and politics – donations and elections – is not as straightforward as critics think. It is pointed out that although a lack of funding can eliminate a candidate from a race, having money even in large quantities does not guarantee success. Researchers for the Campaign Finance Initiative in the US observe that 'If voters do not like what they are hearing, telling them more of the same will not change their opinion.'[9] It is also pointed out that money follows, rather than makes, successful candidates; donors spot the winner and give him money because they have more chance of gaining access in Washington with a likely winner than an uncertain bet. Again, it is claimed that what counts is not the spend itself but the fact that a candidate is attracting lots of donations, because this makes him look like a winner, and the more one looks like a winner the more likely one is to win.

These increasingly influential opinions about the relationship of money and policy in the US may have had their part to play in the thinking behind *Citizens United v. FEC* and *SpeechNOW.org v. FEC* in which the right to freedom of expression by super-PACs was not seen as drowning out, by volume of money, other voices whose right to freedom of expression was effectively thus priced out the market of opinions. But a strong counterargument has come from two political scientists, Martin Gilens of Princeton University and Benjamin Page of Northwestern University, in their 'Testing Theories of American Politics:

Elites, Interest Groups and Average Citizens'.[10] They looked at nearly two thousand government policies enacted over a twenty-year period and correlated them with the policy preferences of both wealthy and average-income citizens. They found that economic elites have a strong impact on policy, average citizens next to none.

> In the United States, our findings indicate, the majority does not rule – at least not in the causal sense of actually determining policy outcomes. When a majority of citizens disagree with economic elites and/or with organized interests, they generally lose. Moreover, because of the strong status quo bias built into the US political system, even when fairly large majorities of Americans favour policy change, they generally do not get it.[11]

These findings are substantiated by a number of other studies. One reported in the *American Journal of Political Science* in 2016 found that politicians were more likely to accept meetings with donors than with non-donors.[12] Another study found a strong correlation between political donations and success in getting government contracts.[13] A book-length examination of the question is Thomas Ferguson's *Golden Rule: The Investment Theory of Party Competition* (1995).[14]

The huge sums of money disbursed in American elections are the price for something. What are they buying? No one will give millions of dollars to political campaigns out of a sense of charity or fun. It is investment, intended to yield a return; it is buying something – access, contracts, favourable tax regimes, exemptions, short-cuts, abolition of expensive environmental regulations or labour protections: the likely shopping list is long. In the UK controls on campaigning spending are tighter, but the Electoral Commission charged with enforcing the limits is relatively toothless, and liable to be inactive unless pushed; it took a private legal action to impel the Electoral Commission to investigate the considerable overspending in the 2016 EU referendum by the Leave campaigns.[15] Overspending in an era of dark money and the electronic means of smuggling it through a vast number of hidden channels distorts the political process severely; therefore while the agencies tasked with protecting the process from fraud and manipulation are weak and ineffective, democracy is held hostage.

And this leads to a final and even more serious problem. Propaganda, spin, undeliverable promises, and outright falsehood have always been the stuff of politics, especially in the run up to elections and referendums. Partisan media of news and opinion have always filled the political debate with polemic, abuse, distortions, and manipulations. But all this has been dangerously weaponized and multiplied by the use of social media as campaigning channels. Conspiracy theories abound on this as on most subjects, but a sober – and sobering – thought puts the matter into perspective, though still a deeply troubling one. This is that elections and referendums are won and lost on small margins. It does not take many to be influenced by deliberate misinformation or disingenuous persuasion to swing the balance in a vote. Profiling and 'micro-targeting' of unsuspecting individuals and groups is standard for the design of advertising that uses social media platforms; data harvesting from the enormous stores of information that exist about social media users, and applied by political campaigners to achieve tailored effects for different groups with different interests, is now the norm.

Consider the example of Cambridge Analytica and its role in the Trump and Brexit campaigns of 2016.[16] By analysing huge amounts of data compiled from social media platforms, Cambridge Analytica constructed detailed psychometric profiles of individuals, enabling it to identify their emotional triggers and to send them tailored campaign messages and advertisements accordingly. The Trump campaign paid Cambridge Analytica over $6 million to influence swing voters in this way. A report in London's Sunday newspaper the *Observer* (26 February 2017) reported the firm's role in the success of the pro-Brexit campaign in the UK; a wealthy individual who funded the Leave campaign said that Cambridge Analytica's 'world class AI had helped them gain unprecedented levels of engagement' among voters, and that 'AI won it for Leave.'[17]

In defence against allegations of being party to a violation of campaign spending limits, Cambridge Analytica claimed that it had provided 'advice' to the Leave campaign 'for free'. The Communications Director of the official Leave campaign told the *Observer* that Robert Mercer, billionaire owner of Breitbart News Network and part-owner of Cambridge Analytica (and a personal friend of leading Brexiters), had offered the company's services to the Leave campaign free of charge because of the 'shared goals' of Breitbart, Trump, and Brexit: 'What they were trying to do in the US and what we were trying to do had massive parallels. We shared a lot of information.'[18]

The *Observer*'s report is instructive:

The strategy involved harvesting data from people's Facebook and other social media profiles and then using machine learning to 'spread' through their networks. [The Communications Director of Leave] admitted the technology and level of information it gathered from people was 'creepy'. He said the campaign used this information, combined with artificial intelligence, to decide who to target with highly individualized advertisements.[19]

It is relevant that no donations of money or services from Cambridge Analytica or Robert Mercer provided to the Leave campaign were filed with the Electoral Commission. An employee of Cambridge Analytica had appeared on a press conference panel to talk about the technology behind the campaign, and the campaign itself had described Cambridge Analytica in its submission to the Electoral Commission as a 'strategic partner'; but when the association between Leave and Cambridge Analytica was made public, Leave wrote to the press to deny that any such association existed. For its own part Cambridge Analytica subsequently refused to comment on whether it donated services to Leave. This coyness on both sides is explained by what the *Observer* next says:

> A leading expert on the impact of technology on elections called the revelation [about the Cambridge Analytica involvement in Leave] 'extremely disturbing and quite sinister'. Professor Martin Moore, of King's College London, said that 'undisclosed support-in-kind is extremely troubling, it undermines the whole bases of our electoral system, that we should have a level playing field' . . . But details of how people were being targeted with this technology raised more serious questions, he said. 'We have no idea what people are being shown or not, which makes it frankly sinister.'[20]

There are several points of concern in this case. The point about transparency is an important one. Everyone is now the subject of profiling and targeting by tailor-made messages as a result; Google not only profiles us on the basis of our internet searches so that it can choose which advertisements to place on the screens of our devices, but it also decides what we might like to know, suited to our individual profile, when we are in search of information. This is troubling enough. But in the case of political campaigns targeting is even less acceptable. Political messaging by its nature is partisan, tendentious, and propagandistic; if it is being expertly fine-tuned to pull our individual 'emotional triggers' it is manipulation of which we are unaware. This is subversion of what should be an open process. If I knew who was targeting me on the basis of a profile of me it had constructed, it would help me to evaluate the messages I was receiving.

So: we have alienation and a sense of disempowerment on the part of voters, worse in electoral systems which effectively disenfranchise many if not most: that is one factor undermining democracy.

We have the toxic combination of careerism – another factor – and organized factionalism in the form of systems of party discipline – a third factor – which makes MPs and Congressmen representatives not of the people but of a party line.

We have as a fourth factor the central and fundamental flaw of the Westminster Model: no separation of powers between executive and legislature in all but the US version, and in this latter the lack of separation between politics and the judiciary. The failure to ensure separation of powers is a dangerous vulnerability, and this danger emerged starkly into daylight in the years immediately before the writing of these words.

We have money placing distorting pressures on polities in favour of the better-off, with increasing inequality – another danger to society: the fifth factor.

And we have the weaponizing and multiplying of the techniques of propaganda, spin, falsehood, and manipulation likewise distorting the political process: the sixth factor.

Each of these factors by itself undermines democracy; any combination of some or all of them demolishes democracy. My claim is that there is no Westminster Model democracy in the world which does not suffer from at least five of these six problems.

CONCLUSION

DEMOCRACY AND
ITS PRINCIPLES

Democracy is a political system in which the people appoint a government and instruct it to legislate and administer on their behalf, protecting and enhancing their interests by responsible and informed action. The concept of democracy requires that we see government as the servant of the people, accountable to them and removable by them if it does not fulfil its function appropriately and adequately.

The nature of democracy and the purposes of democratic government are outlined in the first two chapters of this book. From this explication of the concept of democracy a great deal follows, the following five points in particular.

(1) Democratic government is for *all the people*, not for a group, class, interest, or faction consisting only of some of the people and acting primarily in their interests.

This means (2) that democratic government is neither majoritarian nor minoritarian, but inclusive in its aims, duties, and purposes. Society is a diverse collection of individuals and minorities, and 'a majority' is a more or less temporary coalition of minorities relative to some issue. Democratic government is not majoritarian because not even a large majority can be

165

allowed to overrule minority and individual rights. Democratic government is not minoritarian because a single group or faction in society cannot be allowed to dictate policy, law, and the administration of both, for the totality. When consensus cannot be reached, as often happens given the diversity among minorities, majority agreement is taken as a basis for action unless it violates minority rights, as the rational way forward and in full knowledge that some minorities will be disappointed thereby.

However, despite the reliance on majority agreement when consensus is not reached, the entailment of (1) that government's first duty is to act in the interests of all means that government has in effect to transcend politics, in this sense: that political argument between different parties and interest groups about choices in public policy matters has to be subordinated to the public interest once the people have expressed their preferences, via the ballot box, concerning what they heard in those debates and what they wish to have considered, implemented, or changed.

Because an electoral system (3) giving an accurate reflection of the people's preferences is required, this expression of preferences is likely to result in a legislature in which no single party is larger than all others combined. Accordingly, decisions on policies and laws in the legislature will require agreement among the parties present in it. Compromise and agreement are the way that government rises above partisan political desires. (4) Independent audits of the likely impact of legislation, under a constitutional requirement that the effect on all in the state should be explicitly evaluated, will help to ensure that *government* itself is not *parti pris* but serves the democratic reason for its existence: to serve all and the public good.

The combined effect of these constraints is, to repeat, to elevate government above party politics, which has its appropriate place on the hustings beforehand, in the general national debate at all times, and in the actual formation of government – but not to such an extent in the business of government itself as either to obstruct its duty to the people or render it hostage to partisan interests.

Point (4) is an aspect of the requirement that the duties of government and of legislators and ministers, and the nature, extent, and limits of the functions and powers of the institutions of state and their interrelationships, should be clear and explicit. At least three key components of the state's constitution should be expressly codified: the electoral system and franchise, the rights of all within the borders of the state, and the nature, extent, and limits of the functions and powers of the institutions of government and their interrelationships. The optimal arrangement is that the legislative, executive, and judicial powers should be separate and housed in separate institutions. Since some of the Westminster Model systems are likely to be resistant to reform in this direction, a proportional system of representation will reduce the risk of one-party partisan rule, the current norm in this model, and is therefore the second-best option. In either case, proportional representation is required so that government can be based on cross-party cooperation and agreement rather than leaving it hostage to the more vigorous and ideological actors within a single political party.

Whereas the institutions of government and the means of populating them can be made fully explicit in a constitution whose most significant aspects, at least, are codified, the (5) informal side of the question – the people variously engaged in politics and government, and the news, information, and opinion media – can only be partly regulated by constitutional provisions. The duties and behaviour of representatives might already be set out explicitly in Codes of Conduct, but without full monitoring of representatives' behaviour it is not clear that the mere existence of such codes is adequate; the empirical evidence suggests otherwise. So, because the standards expected of representatives are exigent, monitoring of conformity with such codes should be continuous and searching. Electors have a high responsibility here too, in choosing their representatives; the tendentious role of political activists and party machines in selecting and controlling representatives requires scrutiny and transparency.

Moreover, given the highly partisan nature of much of the press, and the licence provided by social media for every imaginable distortion and falsehood, an independent public fact-checking agency is essential, whose findings should be required to be published on all platforms. The print, broadcast, and social media should be left uncensored but always challengeable, and would in these circumstances be able to disagree with or comment upon the agency's output; but there has to be a resource to which people can turn from the Babel of warring opinions and claims that have vastly proliferated on the internet.

Even the most cursory survey of today's Westminster Model democracies in light of (1)–(5) shows how flawed the model is. Its principal flaw is the absence of a separation of powers, which hugely amplifies the power of the executive, and thereby of anyone or any group with influence in or on the executive. When conjoined with a FPTP voting system it is disastrous.

The UK is a stark example of just how bad the system is. FPTP voting produces a majority in the House of Commons on a minority not just of the electorate as a whole but even of votes cast. The government is formed from this majority of MPs and, through the whipping system of party discipline and career dependency, controls it. The government thereby also controls the business of the House. The House of Lords can delay legislation but not stop it. The executive therefore has total power because Parliament is sovereign, the House of Commons controls Parliament, and the executive controls the majority in the House of Commons. Next, the executive itself is controlled by the most vigorous and partisan minority in the party itself, either directly or via behind-the-scenes pressures and influence, as demonstrated for decades by the rump of anti-EU Conservative MPs who persistently interfered with UK–EU relations by pressure on Conservative governments, and eventually persuaded a Prime Minister to agree to a referendum on the matter – the EU membership referendum of 2016. Thus, a small group of politicians in effect placed a bomb under the wheelhouse of the ship of state, and its detonation caused years of damaging and humiliating debacle for the UK, which plunged rudderless onto the rocks of social and economic dislocation thereafter. In a constitutional order in which the desiderata implied by (1)–(5) obtained, these modern-day Guy Fawkeses would not be able to get anywhere near the wheelhouse to do such harm. They exemplify in the crudest terms *political government*. It is the principal theme of the discussion in this book that *democratic government by its very nature aims to transcend politics* because it is government by the people for the people – and that means all the people. The Westminster Model licenses and promotes government by factions within factions.

The dysfunctional character of the Westminster Model is largely to blame for introducing too much politics into government, and for weaponizing the careerism and factionalism that underlies the adversarial, black-and-white character of debate in Parliament and country. Exacerbated by the FPTP electoral system which entrenches two-party politics and resulting one-party government, the toxins of politics are injected continuously into the bloodstream of US and UK governments, subverting their duty to act in the interests of all with the overall public interest outweighing strictly party-political preferences.

The Westminster Model is inimical to the emergence of statesmen and stateswomen; people of great talent in this regard are lost to their nations by the reduction of politics to the level of a street brawl.[1] In a democracy the sentiment should be that we do not want leaders, we want statesmen and women; we want politics to be a service, not a career; we want the question asked, with respect to every act of the legislature and the executive, 'Does this enhance or at least protect the well-being, security, rights, and prospects of the people?'

Another way of describing matters in Westminster Model polities is that the model represents a stripped-down version and application of an historical truth: that what drives political history is *power cliques*. Not 'ruling classes' but cliques, self-selected and organized to advance an agenda. Marx and others thought in terms of class interests, but to think that a class acts with one mind, except at certain crucial points in defence of a perceived common interest, is to fail to see that *within* each class there are competing interests whose proponents can employ their fellow class-members to advance their own more particular goals. The class itself thus becomes the tool of the clique in it who will obtain the maximum out of their class's dominance.

Democracy is the defence against the usurpation of power by some whose objectives are not coincident with what is optimal for all. Why is FPTP still used in would-be democracies if not to maximize the chances of a faction or clique to gain and exercise control of government? While no one notices that the state's constitutional arrangements conduce to this, this state of affairs will continue. But good constitutional arrangements on the formal *institutional and constitutional* side, and watchfulness and scrutiny on the informal *people, politicians, and press* side, have a chance of promoting the ends of democracy as an order designed to serve all in state and society.

To repeat: government is not the place for politics. Politics is the place for politics: in election campaigns, in the negotiations to form government, in the public debate in general. Democratic government aims at achieving and sustaining the good state; and a good state is one all of whose citizens live in peace and flourish, enjoying rights and freedoms that provide the basis of their flourishing. Recent and contemporary history attests that democracies, or states that aspire to be democratic and which do more than pay lip service to what democracy is supposed to be, come closest to achieving this desideratum, by some margin. Of course, for the reasons given, the world's democracies – let us call them 'near-democracies', especially Westminster Model ones – do not yet achieve flourishing for all their citizens, because social justice and economic inclusion still do not exist in them, as a result of political and economic choices made by those who still get control of the levers respectively of government and economic activity. There are troubling levels of poverty, crime, violence, and suffering in these states therefore. But the fact that the bulk of populations in near-democracies have lives considerably better, by almost all metrics, than their ancestors two or three centuries ago, suggests that the direction of travel is the right one. It would not take much to reform the constitutional arrangements in these states so that the journey to democracy can resume, and more nearly approach its goal.

APPENDIX I:

PROPORTIONAL REPRESENTATION

A central claim in the foregoing is that a *proportionately* representational electoral system – one that adequately reflects the diversity of preferences and interests among the enfranchised – is an essential component of democracy. Proponents of the FPTP system like to say that it results in 'strong government' because it avoids coalitions and messy back-room compromises worked out in smoke-filled rooms. This argument is profoundly disingenuous as regards 'messy compromises and smoke-filled rooms', for every political party is internally a coalition where – far more hidden from public and electoral view – messy compromises are worked out in even smokier rooms. But it also misses the essential point that FPTP ignores the complexity of views in society, disenfranchises whole swathes – indeed, and not untypically, the *majority* of electors – and hands government to one of the competing parties, constituting an oligarchy representing just one of the sets of interests in the nation.

It is a good thing that systems of proportional representation have a tendency to produce coalitions, for coalition-based government – based on compromises and trade-offs – is less likely to result in the application of extreme versions of political ideology to the processes of government. Given that *democratic* government is *for all*, the tendency to politically moderate government has its advantages, in being more Fabian and incremental. But the real virtue is that in coalition there are policy opportunities for interests in society that would simply be blanked in the one-party state that follows a FPTP election.

There are various systems of proportional representation – I shall not rehearse the technicalities of these varieties here – and they all have to address the dilemma of Arrow's 'Impossibility Theorem' in social choice theory, which states that there is no way of arriving at an ordering of alternatives chosen by a set of rational and autonomous people holding different ordering preferences.[1] However, two considerations render the Arrow dilemma less than fatal to the idea of choices among more than two options: the first is that voters are not as a group 'rational and autonomous' in the required theoretical sense, and the second is that there is no expectation of *perfection* in the outcome of a choice mechanism, only that it should approximate more than acceptably to the aim of securing a just and representative portrayal of the spread of preferences in an electorate. Several among the varieties of proportional representation systems achieve this well, and take a polity far closer to the entailments of the concept of democracy than the FPTP system.

Objectors to proportional representation urge the importance of the link between representatives (Congressmen and women, MPs) and their constituents. This is part piety, part good point. It is a piety because congressional districts in the US represent over 700,000 people on average, while constituencies in the UK contain about 70,000 people on average, so no personal link between an individual representative and the overwhelming majority of these constituents is possible. Representatives will tell you that a small posse of persistent constituents will appear with regularity at their offices or 'constituency surgeries', and they will also – if frank – acknowledge the relative powerlessness of the individual representative to do anything about the problems – housing, access to health care, loss of welfare payments, and the like – that bedevil some they represent; or even to do much in response to the lobbying from businesses and other organizations seeking planning permission, an input into taxation policy, grants, and the like again. On the other hand, it is of value to constituents to know the name or names of those who represent their area in the legislature; but FPTP is not the only way to ensure this. There is no inconsistency between linking representatives to constituencies and electing them by a fair and genuinely *representative* system of voting.

Achieving a fair and representative portrayal of the spread of preferences among the enfranchised is not the only requirement. A second and very important one is that the electoral system should not result in very small parties in the legislature holding government to ransom because the balance of power rests with them. This is frequently observed in the Israeli and Italian systems. One way to obviate this is by a minimum percentage vote to secure representation – 5% of votes cast is a generous such threshold – and a second and supplementary way is to have constitutional provisions that certain central responsibilities of government (principally, budgetary and security matters) cannot be delayed too long by the objections of a minority of the legislature *below* a certain percentage of representatives.

The associated argument that a proportional system allows undesirable extremist small parties into the legislature, invites the following points in reply. First, if such a party secures a percentage of the vote, that is an indication that there is a group in society that seeks representation, and in a democracy they have a right to be heard – provided that their opinions are not aimed at inciting violence, discrimination, or hate – even if most others do not like their message. Secondly and more importantly, allowing such opinions to be vented and then discussed and challenged in the legislature is a way of defusing their destabilizing potential in society where, if they are outside the institutions of the polity, they can profit from marginalization and grow as cankers do, infecting the body politic – for it is a fact, all the more potent in the era of social media, that movements outside the state's political institutions can make far more noise, and occupy a far larger arc of the public horizon, than their numbers actually warrant. If they are in the legislature on the basis of a system of proportional representation, their true size and reach is immediately obvious, and they are less of a threat as a result.

It is in any case undemocratic in principle to argue that (outside incitements to violence, discrimination, and hate) there are views that should not be allowed representation in society. This is related to an objection that anti-democrats sometimes urge, which is that it is a challengeable assumption of democracy that because a majority want X they must have X, however damaging or unwise from an objective standpoint X might be. The rejoinder, But who says that X is damaging or unwise? Who speaks more authoritatively on the matter than the majority? is regarded as settling the matter on the very same ground – viz. that majority will is enough. Let us remember but here leave aside the fact that majority will cannot prevail over minority rights, and note that, as a separate matter, an anti-democrat might in response ask a pertinent question: Why does the majority want X? Could they have been misinformed, do they believe a falsehood, are they acting on questionable

176

impulses such as xenophobia? Then there is the question, *Should* they want X? – in the sense (for example) of '*is it wise* to want to smoke tobacco, drink large quantities of alcohol, drive too fast on the highway?' For how is it tolerable – the anti-democrat will conclude – to accept that merely wanting X in large enough numbers outweighs better-informed, more expert, or more considered judgment about the value of X?

The concept of *representative democracy* is the reply to these challenges. It is a system designed to serve the interests of all by getting and acting upon the relevant information about what would serve those interests – for example, instituting a public education system, providing hospitals and trained medical personnel, maintaining a trained army for defence, and so on. Representatives are elected – and thereafter employed – to do a job requiring informed judgment, just as medical doctors, airline pilots, and teachers are. The point was emphatically made in the foregoing that, given that this is so, electors must be careful to send *good* representatives to the legislature, not least because we are licensing them to take decisions that we individually might not agree with (raising the level of taxation, for example).

But electors must also know that, unless they are members of a very small outlier group in society, their expression of policy preference will register in the overall governance of their society, and that this must feed into the informed judgment – as part of the information, indeed – that representatives must make. For this, as for participation and inclusion in general, a proportional system of representation is essential.

It is arguably the case that the events of the significant year 2016, in which Donald Trump was elected US President and a referendum in the United Kingdom yielded a result which allowed proponents of Brexit to claim the right to pursue their

policy, illustrate how FPTP has begun to devour its own proponents. Thus: FPTP entrenches two-party politics. Each party
has to satisfy its 'base': a party of the right – business and the
better-off; a party of the left – working people and the disadvan-
taged (speaking roughly in both cases). But neither base by itself
is enough to secure a majority in the legislature, a problem
somewhat more severe for the right than the left, although the
left has a problem competing with the right on election funding.
Consider the Republican Party in the US as a key example. Its
base is corporate America, which does not have enough votes to
secure a majority in Congress or to win a presidential election,
so it resorts to populist measures to secure those votes: opposing immigration, tapping into racism in the Southern states,
gathering Catholic and evangelical Christian votes by opposing
abortion, securing the votes and funds of the gun lobby, and so
on. In the decades since the 1950s American politics has moved
rightwards more and more as these tropes have come to dominate the discourse of political campaigning. The Democrats in
the US have had to move rightwards along with them, following
the shifting centre of political gravity. Today's US Democrats
look like 1950s Republican moderates; today's Republicans are
indistinguishable from the Tea Party extremists of the turn of
the early twenty-first century.

In the UK the same process has repeated itself, with minor
variations: as the Conservative Party in the UK became indistinguishable from the Brexit Party so a socialist leadership of the
Labour Party – still wedded to ideas that failed in the 1960s and
70s, and repudiating the rightward-shifted and thus more 'moderate' position known as 'Blairism' which saw a long period of
largely successful centre-left government between 1997 and
2010 – tried to occupy a position that was no longer electorally
tenable, and had in certain respects come to be indistinguishable

from the right-wing populism that led to the post-2016 constitutional crisis in the UK – supporting Brexit, equivocating on immigration, falling foul of claims of anti-Semitism.

Had the FPTP electoral system operative in each case not created the undemocratically elected and intrinsically undemocratic limitation to just two political alternatives, this polarizing drift towards more extreme political positions would have been far less likely to happen. The more extreme political positioning at which the US and UK arrived in 2016 involved or threatened openly anti-democratic expedients: for striking examples President Trump's 'war on the Constitution'[2] and repeated efforts by UK proponents of Brexit to bypass or game Parliament in order to get their way.[3]

Two-party politics, entrenched by FPTP, has increasingly resorted to populist expedients; populism is threatening to destroy the polities themselves, like the monster that turns on its creator – Frankenstein, the Golem.

The solution is: proportional representation, and reassertion of the representative principle under clear constitutional constraints.

APPENDIX II:

ALTERNATIVE FORMS
OF DEMOCRACY

The foregoing premises the concept of *representative democracy* and argues for ways to make it work in satisfaction of the demands implicit in the concept of democracy itself. This premise (of *representative* democracy as the most effective system) is not accepted by many critics of current standard forms of democracy, who argue instead for alternatives: direct democracy, sortition, and 'deliberative democracy' chief among them. Versions of these views are native also to anarchism as a serious and thought-out approach to social governance, which repudiates the idea of the state altogether and argues for voluntary, self-governing, cooperative, non-state societies. It might be argued that anarchism – understood as rejection of the concept of overarching authority to which individuals and communities are subject – provides the most natural framework for these alternative forms of democracy. To evaluate them, some comments on anarchism are accordingly a useful place to start.

Anarchist views are predicated on definitions of the state as the entity holding a monopoly on force. On conventional views, keeping order in society and confronting crime requires organized policing, and defence against threat from without requires trained armed services; these are the state's instruments of force, and it has to be the sole agent licensed to use them. In populous and complex societies the need for organization generates bureaucracies and hierarchies. Couple force with hierarchy, regard this junction as malign – as it has been and still is in many places; think Gestapo, KGB, Stasi – and the anxieties that prompt a preference for anarchism make themselves clear.

The premise that structures of organization, and the need for protection against crime and threat, are either *intrinsically* – just in their nature – or *dangerously prone* to being malign is required for anarchism. But this premise is as obviously false as it is obviously true that the existence of both can indeed be turned to malign purposes. In advanced democracies the response to this latter fact is to institute regimes of rights, and to demand transparency in all organs of state with the understood exception of those security services attempting to protect the state against acts of terrorism or espionage and therefore requiring to work outside the public gaze. Their inaccessibility to the public gaze does not mean they are unanswerable to the organs of government responsible for them.

A better argument for anarchism is that the machineries of state cannot but operate in ways liable to crush in their cogs those who trip as they attempt to make their way through life's complexities and difficulties. Large bureaucracies find it hard to respond in individually sensitive ways to nuanced and complicated individual circumstances. Far better, then, argues the anarchist, for people to organize themselves into voluntary cooperatives, governing themselves by agreement, without an overarching force-monopolizing authority to compel compliance and conformity.

This utopian idea is attractive, but it requires a different and even less persuasive premise: that human nature is typically apt for the voluntary cooperation that anarchists advocate. The premise is supported by the undoubted fact that humans are social beings, who usually flourish best when in relationships with others, and display natural instincts of sympathy, concern, and need for others in those relationships. But it ignores the preference that individuals have for kin over strangers, for their own survival and self-interest over the survival or interest of individuals unknown to them, of propensities among some to be free-riders on others' endeavours, and the propensities for greed, aggression, and cruelty that humans too often display. And it ignores the very important fact that resources have to be copious enough, or needs modest and restrained enough, for the usual causes of competition and conflict to be avoided.

There is, interestingly, a classic debate in Chinese philosophy about whether human nature is innately good or bad.[1] Confucius and his successor Mencius were emphatically of the view that human nature is fundamentally good. A less optimistic opinion was held by the third master of the Confucian tradition, Xunzi. Mencius explained wrongdoing as the result of external forces; in hard times people turn to crime or violence because they are struggling to survive. It is not natural for people to be like that, he wrote, but suffering 'sinks and drowns their hearts'. As proof of innate goodness Mencius cites such phenomena as the distress anyone feels on seeing a child in danger; we do not feel distress because we wish to please the child's parents or to get social approval; the sentiment arises in our *xin*, our hearts. On this view, equitable socio-economic circumstances together with natural human sociability would provide the conditions suitable for voluntary cooperation among people without need for overarching force-monopolizing government.

Xunzi thought very differently. In his view people are by nature inclined to be bad; being good, he said, takes conscious effort. People are basically greedy; they seek personal profit; they see others as rivals, and therefore envy and hostility arise, and that causes crime, violence, and betrayal. People are naturally endowed to seek pleasure in preference to virtue if the latter makes laborious or painful demands, which it often does. Therefore, Xunzi wrote, education is necessary, and with it the provision of models of upright behaviour. Only then do 'courtesy, refinement and loyalty' develop. He wrote: 'Thus, a warped piece of wood requires the press-frame, steam to soften it, and force applied to straighten it. A blunt piece of metal must be whetted on the grindstone to make it sharp.'[2] In short, there has to be enforceable authority to protect people from the greed, rivalry, and self-interest of other people.

It is agreeable to think that the truth lies somewhat more with Confucius and Mencius than with Xunzi, and it probably does; but it lies enough with Xunzi to make anarchism too Utopian a project. The forms of democracy proposed as alternatives to representative democracy to a greater or lesser degree rely on the same premises assumed by anarchists, and suffer the same criticisms of these therefore. One need only regard Xunzi's view as partially true to think that protecting the weak against the strong cannot be left to the goodwill of neighbours only, but requires organization to provide it and efficacy in delivering it.

This is so even in the one circumstance identified by Rousseau in his *Social Contract* (1762) where democracy has the best chance of working: the very simple small state whose citizens are basically equal in wealth and status, who know each other personally, and who can readily assemble, all together, to debate and decide matters. He here reprises the Aristotelian idea that the perfect state is a community whose size is limited by the audible reach of the stentor's voice when he shouts news, warnings, or a summons to the agora. Against this idyllic-seeming

view of the small, self-determining, truly democratic community might be urged the disadvantages of what is – in effect –
village life, which according to its more acidulous observers can
at its worst be an arena of parochialism, triviality, gossip, jealous-
ies, rivalries, interference, and the coercions of social disapproval and persecution – these latter identified by Mill as being
every bit as bad as political tyranny. That what one might call
'toxic village syndrome' can indeed exist is a question-mark over
the utopian vision of the perfect small democracy or the self-
governing cooperative.

And in any self-organizing group of human beings, personality becomes a dominant factor. In various circumstances someone more confident and assertive, or physically bigger, or louder,
or angrier, or more subtle and designing, or cleverer, or more
ambitious, will quickly emerge into a leadership role. Two or
more such will sooner or later clash. If everyone is in charge,
disagreements will multiply. In the utopian vision, all in the
community sensibly agree a set of arrangements and a distribution of responsibilities, and peaceful flourishing follows.
Historical experience shows that near-peaceful flourishing is
more likely when such arrangements are formalized and means
of maintaining their operation exist – together with means of
changing them, when necessary, by a due process itself accepted
by all. This, in short, is the state. And one virtue of a *democratic*
state is that it is most capable of insuring against 'domination' in
Ian Shapiro's sense of this term, as mentioned in chapter I.[3]

These thoughts challenge not just anarchism but also the idea
of direct democracy on the small scale, but do such considerations apply on a somewhat larger scale? An interesting example
of a system approaching direct democracy is offered by
Switzerland. Switzerland's governments are always multi-party
coalitions which, on matters of significance where there is

insufficient consensus within the governing coalition itself, employ the device of frequent referendums to decide matters. This gives citizens a degree of participation and power which, as admirers of the system note, is unparalleled in other democracies. Critics of the Swiss system, however, say that the result is low turnouts and notably conservative decisions. The divisiveness of referendums – inviting polarization and psychological investment in the polarity chosen – sometimes holds the country in thrall; French-speaking and German-speaking Swiss disagree across the *Röstigraben* – the 'hash potato divide'[4] – over a range of issues, most especially the European Union, which most French Swiss wish to join and most German Swiss do not.

It is claimed by defenders of the Swiss system that the Swiss are assiduous in doing their homework on what is at stake in referendums; the frequent resort to them makes citizens more responsible in their approach to them. Because Switzerland is a relatively small, highly educated, and prosperous state (the total population at eight million is slightly less than that of London, its GDP per capita is over $80,000 per annum compared to the UK's $39,700 and the US's $59,500) this is plausible, and arguably is as much the result as the cause of the intelligent approach taken to referendum questions. Indeed the question of size is possibly the most significant factor; more populous states wishing to emulate the success of the Swiss model would do well to consider devolving government regionally as close as possible to the size enjoyed by the successful examples of Switzerland, Norway, Denmark, and Sweden, all with populations below ten million and all with GDP per capita levels higher than the UK.[5] In populations of this size and smaller, the chance of developing thoughtful forms of more direct democracy seems greater, not least because of the opportunity for more deliberative policy processes in them, correlated with effective citizen participation and consultation – perhaps, as one main idea suggests, in citizen assemblies, perhaps also convened by sortition.

The question is whether there is an optimal population size for this to be possible, and whether that is indeed in the region of ten million or below.[6] It might be that in states with populations of twenty, fifty, three hundred million, a billion or more, representative democracy is the default. If so, there is no reason why it cannot be made to function well, as the foregoing chapters argue.

However, consider first the following lesson. The idea of democracy, as noted already, was regarded with opprobrium until recently in history. Alternatives to monarchy, especially in its absolutist form, were proposed under various guises, a form of constitutionalism winning in the 1688 settlement in England, thereafter leading to the great American developments at the end of the eighteenth century and eventuating in qualified forms of democracy itself, at least in the Eurocentric world, in the nineteenth and twentieth centuries. Representative systems have been the main outcome.

But it is worth noting that some of the alternative ideas that seem attractive to contemporary proponents of more direct and participatory forms of democracy were anticipated a number of times in the debate in and since the seventeenth century, a debate itself harking back to proto-democratic practices in classical times. One such occurs in James Harrington's Oceana (1656) which, although not advocating democracy as directly as the Levellers did – recall the Putney Debates of 1647 and the 'Agreement of the People' there put forward, calling for universal male suffrage – and although insisting on the relationship between the franchise and land-ownership, nevertheless proposed a form of democratic participation which Harrington borrowed from the Roman republican experience of power-sharing between the senatorial class and the plebeians, whose tribunes exercised powers of veto over Senate decisions. This contains several interesting anticipations of contemporary suggestions for citizen participation, as follows.

In the Roman republic 'power lay in the people, authority in the Senate', as Cicero put it. Rome's senators were astute enough to recognize that popular consent was a condition of government. It was secured through the institution of the tribunate. Although the Consuls were the chief officers of state, these being two men chosen each year as joint prime ministers, the people's representatives – the 'tribunes of the people' – had substantial powers. Elected by the plebeians, they could propose laws and had a veto over Senate-initiated legislation. Their duty was to represent the interests of the ordinary citizens. Polybius wrote, 'The tribunes are bound to do what the people resolve and chiefly to focus on their wishes.'[7] The system lasted until Augustus Caesar became emperor after the civil war, absorbing the powers of the tribunate in his own person, and it so remained with all Roman emperors thereafter.

This republican model attracted Harrington. In his *Oceana* (by which he meant England as he thought it should be, and would be if reformed) he quoted Livy's 'rule of law, not of men', and proceeded to outline a system of governance which reprised, but with significant adaptations, some of the Roman themes. His model is as follows. Power should be shared by property-owners, though how much property anyone can own should be limited so that ownership can be as widespread as possible. In addition to producing a strong and flourishing middle class this would prevent over-accumulation of wealth in too few hands, for divergence between economic and political power is, he wrote, a danger to the state. Property-owners should constitute a Senate which proposes laws, and the laws should be put to the people for ratification. Once ratified, the laws should be put into effect by magistrates, who are elected for limited terms so that as many people as possible can have a turn in the magistracy. In addition to rotation of elected officials, Harrington proposed that there should be popular assemblies at all levels from parishes upwards to the national level.

Note the suggestions in this for local, regional, and national assemblies, with power of decision over laws vested in the people; election of term-limited magistrates (that is, the officials of the executive branch of government); the spread of wealth and ownership widely through society; and his warnings about the dangers of inequality. Today the idea of reserving the power of initiating legislation to property-owners only, even on Harrington's more egalitarian basis, is not acceptable – and for the reason given by Harrington's contemporary, Thomas Rainsborough, namely, that every citizen has a right to a voice, independently of wealth and property, not just in approving but in framing the laws. But the other suggestions are distinctively like contemporary theories of alternative democratic orders.

And now we note that England in Harrington's day had a population of five million; Rome at the end of the republican period, in Cicero's day, between one and two million. In both cases – though more so in seventeenth-century England than in first-century BCE Rome – communications were slow and literacy levels modest. Today's Norway and Switzerland – again to use them as examples of successful democratic societies – have instant communications and almost total literacy. Although ease of communication and high levels of literacy have to be factors in the advantages of more direct forms of democracy, the size factor again obtrudes itself as significant. Once the population of a state increases beyond the size of Norway and Switzerland it becomes less plausible to see

Harrington-style suggestions working, unless there is very significant regional devolution.

One obvious reason for this is that in more populous societies the fact that government operates at a distance from people in their daily lives gives rise to feelings of individual powerlessness. With remoteness comes detachment; people do not feel that they are involved in conferring legitimacy on government, nor that they can trust it fully. Greater participation and a greater sense of genuinely having an effect are clearly desirable. This is achieved by party-political activism; but not everyone, perhaps not the majority, want to be involved in that way, for there is a difference between engaging in party politics and engaging in decision-making – the difference, often, between ideology and pragmatism, gnosis and praxis.

In most Western states participatory activities outside political activism have in fact increased in the first decades of the twenty-first century, precisely in response to the increasingly felt remoteness of national government.[8] Citizens' assemblies, and – for decisions about major change – constitutional conventions, figure among the major suggestions put forward for such activity. There are already-existing local forums whose greater use for the same purpose could be valuable: for example, public attendance at and involvement in municipal meetings, and frequent 'town-halls' in the American manner at which officials and politicians, both local and national, are questioned by citizens. These would be among the mechanisms of an anarchy as the instruments for cooperative self-government, but they could supplement and give greater legitimacy and content to representative democracy too.

The apparent move towards greater citizen participation in the form of referendums and petitions in the UK can be viewed either as a gradual acceptance that the gap between government and citizen has grown too great, or – as a sceptic might see it – as a sop to the demand for more consultation. In Switzerland a referendum can be triggered by a petition of 1.2% of the population; in one salient UK case, a petition signed by over six million people (nearly 10% of the population) was ignored by the government.[9] At certain levels of support UK petitions trigger parliamentary debates – these are typically held with a few MPs present in St Stephen's Hall in Westminster, not on the floor of the House of Commons itself, in the view of sceptics thus making a mockery of the petition process, and showing it to be cosmetic rather than a serious response to the demand for participation.

What then are the prospects for greater participation in populous democracies? A leading advocate of deliberative democracy is James Fishkin, a Stanford University professor of communication and political science, who directs the Stanford Center for Deliberative Democracy.[10] In his applied model, called 'deliberative polling', a representative sample of the citizenry is brought together to discuss a given topic, provided with briefing materials carefully prepared to avoid bias, and encouraged to consider and debate conscientiously, giving all points of view their due attention and focusing on the arguments and not on who puts them forward. They then vote. The model has been applied in a variety of countries including South Korea, Brazil, Bulgaria, and Northern Ireland, and in a number of cases the views of participants were significantly changed as a result of the experience.[11]

This was experimental work, but critics might quickly point out that however deliberative the process, it is still polling; these are focus groups, small samples of the population however carefully they match the whole population in their range across age, sex, ethnicity, and income and educational level. Opinion polls and focus groups might have a degree of influence on policy decisions, and almost certainly a larger degree of influence on politicians' anxieties, but as means of *legitimizing* policy they fall far short of a vote of all the enfranchised.

Almost all the examples given in the chapter entitled 'Bringing Power Closer to the People' in a report by the UK's Electoral Reform Society in 2019[12] were of efforts along these lines, although one raised the problem from a different direction. This was the institution of a permanent citizen body, chosen by lottery, in the German-speaking part of Belgium, to make policy proposals to the regional Parliament.[13] The body, known as the 'Citizens Council', has twenty-four members drafted by lot, as in jury service. Here the question arises of the democratic authority of the Citizens' Council vis-à-vis the Parliament. Drawn by lot from the populace, it has the same degree of authority that a Parliament constituted by sortition would have, or that a jury has. Is it in competition with the Parliament, therefore? The Parliament is elected by voters on the basis of what candidates offered in their manifestos before polling day. Can citizens' councillors chosen randomly have the same imprimatur from the people as the Members of Parliament?

The problem of competing democratic authority is sharpest in the case of having two Houses of Congress or Parliament elected on the same basis as each other. In the UK, a directly elected House of Lords would be in competition with the House of Commons in its claim to speak for the people. 'Gridlock' occurs sufficiently often in the US Congress to show that without clear constitutional means of adjusting which democratic imprimatur outweighs which other democratic imprimatur, trouble is bound to ensue. The same problem arises with citizen assemblies, whether constituted by election or sortition. Suppose they are at sharp variance with the Congress or Parliament; what would that be a recipe for?

The fact is that an elected Congress or Parliament is *the* citizen body *par excellence* – it is supposed to be, and constitutionally is, *the* deliberative forum, with the added significance that it is constitutionally charged with deciding on the laws of the state and (more rather than less notionally in Westminster Model democracies) holding the executive to account in its administration of those laws. Everything from focus groups to citizen assemblies are minor duplications of this, even if they could be argued to be more genuinely representative of the population at large given that they have been especially selected so to be. In this respect, indeed, they would not be without their usefulness in creating greater understanding of, and feedback on, issues of the day; they would certainly draw more citizens into engagement with matters of government. In states of optimal population size, this process could replace or be a constitutional adjunct to aiding the work of the elected legislature and executive. But in populous states the mechanisms of legislation and government have to be based on the active conferment of authority by the enfranchised in the electoral process. That process, and the institutions that emerge from it, have to conform to the implications of the concept of *democracy* as discussed in the foregoing chapters.

Representation was discussed in chapter 1, and there contrasted with the alternative forms discussed here. The points merit repeating. Direct democracy is not representative because it does not require to be so; sortition constitutes the legislature randomly, by lottery, as in jury service, and is thus not intended to be representative, but to act as an enlarged standing opinion poll sample; cellular democracy involves a highly indirect form of representation in that assemblies at different levels from local through regional to national each send delegates to the level above. The first and second forms of democracy invite the familiar Platonic strictures about the degree of knowledge, aptness, altruism, and long-termism that legislatures thus populated would exhibit, given that these characteristics would seem to be required for the production of at least good-enough government. Advocates of direct democracy would appeal to the wisdom of the masses in reply, and advocates of sortition would reply that a randomly selected body of legislators would not perform much worse than a body of career politicians, and perhaps better – especially if, as with juries, appointment were for a set term so that participants would have no vested interest in anything other than doing their best, with no career ambitions or party-political pressures operating upon them. The third suggestion attenuates the connection between the enfranchised and government far more than the familiar systems of representation in most contemporary democracies, and it attracts scepticism accordingly.

These thoughts, in conjunction with those expressed above, suggest that at least in more populous states the system of representative democracy remains the best, on these conditions: if the electoral system is properly representative, a separation of powers exists or, as second best, the electoral system yields coalition government based on trans-party agreement predicated on the national interest, and the constitutional arrangements define clearly the nature and limits of the powers and duties of legislature and executive.

The alternative is regionalism, which has much to recommend it from the point of view of citizen engagement in democratic processes, though the risk is loss of the advantages of scale, such as economies of scale, that larger national units provide. Federalism offers a partial solution, if the dispersal and sharing of powers at the regional and federal levels are satisfactorily arranged and in ways that preserve the desideratum of greater citizen participation in the political and governmental processes.

On a realistic note, it has to be acknowledged that many people, and probably the majority of them, do not wish to be bothered with matters of politics and governments too frequently, still less unremittingly. They certainly wish to be the final authority in the state along with their fellow citizens, and to have their voices heard as such; but they have their lives, careers, families, and other concerns to deal with, and therefore send people to the legislature and executive in the expectation that they will do a competent job on their behalf. Devising ways of bringing political influence closer to the people is a worthy ideal, but it carries the risk that it simply places that influence into the hands of self-selected activists and zealots. Representative democracy charges those who are elected in the statutory procedure for election with a responsibility for which they are accountable: that is the way this aspect of democracy needs to be conducted. The alternatives, from anarchy to the other proposals put forward, add both burdens and insecurities to citizenship which the formal structures of governance are intended to mitigate. That is why representative democracy recommends itself so strongly.

APPENDIX III:

SOME WESTMINSTER MODEL SYSTEMS

The following states have Westminster Model systems, or governance systems closely based upon it. Some have continued to be monarchies (with Queen Elizabeth II of the United Kingdom on the throne)[1] and some have become republics.

Westminster Model states which are monarchies with Queen Elizabeth as Head of State: Antigua and Barbuda, Australia, Bahamas, Barbados, Belize, Bermuda, Canada, Grenada, New Zealand, Papua New Guinea, St Kitts and Nevis, St Lucia, St Vincent and the Grenadines, Solomon Islands, Tuvalu, United Kingdom.

Westminster Model systems with their own monarchs: Japan, Kuwait, Malaysia.

Westminster Model systems which are republics: Bangladesh, Dominica, India, Ireland, Israel, Malta, Mauritius, Pakistan, Singapore, Trinidad and Tobago, United States of America, Vanuatu.

Systems which were formally the Westminster Model and have evolved from it: Burma, Fiji, Gambia, Ghana, Guyana, Kenya, Malawi, Nigeria, Sierra Leone, South Africa, Sri Lanka, Swaziland, Tanzania, Uganda, Zambia, Zimbabwe.

Countries that use the FPTP electoral system (note how many are British in origin and overlap with the above lists): Antigua and Barbuda, Azerbaijan, Bahamas, Bangladesh, Barbados, Belize, Bermuda, Bhutan, Botswana, Brazil, Canada, Cayman Islands, Cook Islands, Côte d'Ivoire, Dominica, Eritrea, Ethiopia, Gabon, Gambia, Ghana, Grenada, India, Indonesia, Jamaica, Kenya, Kuwait, Laos, Liberia, Malawi, Malaysia, Maldives, Marshall Islands, Mauritius, Micronesia, Myanmar, Nigeria, Niue, Oman, Pakistan, Palau, Philippines, Poland, St Kitts and Nevis, St Lucia, St Vincent and the Grenadines, Samoa, Seychelles, Sierra Leone, Singapore, Solomon Islands, Swaziland (Eswatini), Taiwan, Tanzania, Tonga, Trinidad and Tobago, Tuvalu, Uganda, United Kingdom, United States of America, Virgin Islands, Yemen, Zambia.

Countries without a codified constitution: Canada, Israel, New Zealand, San Marino, Saudi Arabia, United Kingdom.

Australia has a bicameral legislature consisting of a House of Representatives with 150 members, and a Senate with seventy-six members. Members of the lower house are elected for three-year terms, each of them representing an electoral division. Members of the Senate are elected for six years if representing one of the six states in the Commonwealth, or three years if representing one of the Commonwealth's two territories. Each state returns twelve senators, the two territories two each. Like the US Senate, the Australian Senate is a 'states' house'; the number of senators is not proportional to the population of the state.

As is fundamental to the Westminster Model, the government is formed from the majority in the House of Representatives. The Governor-General of Australia – the Queen's representative in the country – appoints as Prime

Minister whoever commands majority support in the lower house. All government ministers must be members of the Parliament; the Constitution in effect mandates that there be no separation of powers between executive and legislature. A cabinet comprised of senior ministers is the effective decision-making body in government, though the Constitution provides for a Federal Executive Council chaired by the Governor-General on which all ministers sit *ex officio*. The Council appoints High Court judges.

The electoral system in Australia has several distinctive features. One is compulsory voting, including compulsory enrolment on the electoral register.[2] The House of Representatives is elected on a majority-preferential instant run-off system, while the Senate is elected by a single transferable vote proportional system. The system used for electing the lower house reproduces a two-party effect by allocating votes to the two principal candidates in each district. The two blocs between which the choice thus effectively lies is, on the one hand, the right-of-centre coalition between the Liberal Party and the National Party, and, on the other hand, the centre-left Labour Party. The electoral system for the House of Representatives unluckily produces the same effect as a plurality FPTP system, though there is slightly more chance of representation for minor parties than in the latter.

Canada's system cleaves closely to the Westminster Model, including its reliance on the unwritten conventions and traditions of the uncodified Westminster constitution. Its House of Commons has 338 members elected by FPTP in single-member constituencies known as 'ridings'. The longest permissible period between elections is five years. Members of the Senate are appointed by the Governor-General to serve until the age of seventy-five. Notionally the Senate is regionally representative, though over time it has become less reliably so. In most respects Canada reprises the system in the UK, with the added complication of the state's federal structure and the diversity among the provinces, from natural-resources-rich far west through industrial centre to relatively poor east, and with many in the French-speaking province of Quebec perennially uncomfortable with their membership of the federation. It is a question of how the Westminster Model order sustains this polity; on the one hand it might be that its Heath Robinson nature suits the assorted nature of the state itself; on the other hand it is likely that when clarity, consistency, and a robust framework for absorbing political shocks are required, the system will be found wanting.

India, the world's most populous democracy, has a bicameral Parliament. Its upper house, the Rajya Sabha, is 'the Council of States' and the lower house, the Lok Sabha, is 'the House of the People'. The Rajya Sabha has 245 members, 233 elected by the state assemblies for six-year terms, a further twelve appointed by the President. One-third of the membership retires every two years. The Lok Sabha has 545 members, of whom 543 are elected by FPTP in constituencies across the country's states and territories. Two seats are allocated for the Anglo-Indian community. Nearly a quarter of the seats are reserved for 'Scheduled Castes' and 'Scheduled Tribes'. Suffrage is universal and elections are required to be held every five years or less.

The Lok Sabha's members elect the Prime Minister, and he or she appoints a Council of Ministers. The President is elected for a five-year term by an Electoral College drawn from elected representatives in the federal Parliament and the state assemblies. Legislation can be initiated in either house, but final authority over financial matters lies with the Lok Sabha. The Prime Minister and all ministers are required to be members of one of the Houses of Parliament; anyone appointed to a ministerial position has to seek membership of one of the Houses within six months. Like Australia, therefore, conflation of the executive and legislative powers is required by the constitution.

New Zealand became a unicameral system in 1951 by abolishing its upper house, the Legislative Council. In 1996 it modified its FPTP electoral system by means of a mixed-member proportional system, in which Members of Parliament are elected either in single-member constituencies by FPTP or from a party list. The Parliament has 120 seats, although the electoral system sometimes produces more or fewer than this. Seven seats are reserved for representatives on a separate Maori electoral register, although Maoris can stand for election on the general register or a party list also. Elections are held every three years.

The modified electoral system typically yields no majority for any one party, thus favouring coalition government. All ministers are required to be Members of Parliament. The Governor-General, representing the Queen, appoints as Prime Minister the person who can command a majority in the Parliament. Here too, true to the Westminster arrangement, executive and legislature consist of the same people, but in light of the electoral system and ensuing coalitions, the negative effects of this are diluted.

The USA separates the executive and legislative powers, with an executive President elected by an Electoral College and, separately, a bicameral legislature consisting of a House of Representatives and a Senate. The Senate is a states' house, with each state electing two senators irrespective of the number of voters in the state. There are accordingly 100 senators. This is the result of the 'Great Compromise' or 'Connecticut

Compromise' reached in 1787 to protect the interests of individual states joining the federal union. In US constitutional
orthodoxy the federal government 'shares sovereignty' with the
states, although the nature of the relationship is a matter of
contention which flares into controversy at times.

Election of the 435 members of the House of Representatives
is by FPTP in single-member congressional districts. Because of
the widespread and longstanding practice of gerrymandering –
arranging the boundaries of congressional districts to favour a
given party – the majority of congressional seats never change
hands.[3] Elections occur every two years for the House of
Representatives, and for one-third of the Senate; senators' terms
are six years. Members of Congress are not allowed to serve in
the government; the President appoints his administration from
outside Congress.

Despite the FPTP electoral system for the House of
Representatives, the unrepresentative nature of the Senate, and
the Electoral College arrangement for the Presidency which
increasingly in recent times results in Presidents taking office on
a minority of the popular vote, the US can be regarded as a
country positively drunk on democracy, in that in addition to
the federal and state legislatures and executives – the states
having a variety of systems of their own – there are nearly 90,000
local government bodies, with elected representatives and officials for counties, municipalities, school districts, fire authorities, sheriffs, judges (in some places), and more. Public provision such as education, health, policing, transport, and sanitation
are dealt with at municipal and state levels, and cities have
elected mayors or professional managers hired by the elected
city council. Arguably, therefore, there is too little genuine
democracy where it matters, and sometimes too much where
qualified appointments would be an advantage – a fact

implicitly recognized in the appointment of professional town managers where this occurs.

Elections in the US are expensive for candidates, and money is a large and distorting factor in American democracy: see chapter 8.

Justices of the Supreme Court are appointed by the President subject to confirmation by the Senate, constituting a failure of the separation of powers in a very crucial respect, with major effects on the character of American life and society.

South Africa is frequently cited as an example of a state that has modified its Westminster system, but on examination one sees that the degree of modification is modest from the point of view of structure, though innovative with regard to the electoral system. There is a bicameral Parliament consisting of a 400-member National Assembly and a ninety-member upper house called the National Council of Provinces, which – as its name suggests – is a states' house, its members elected by the nine provincial assemblies.

The National Assembly is elected every five years on a party list system of proportional representation, half the members from nine provincial lists and half from national lists, seats in the Assembly being allocated on the proportion of votes cast for each party. The President, a sitting Member of Parliament, is elected by the Members of Parliament and appoints ministers from among other sitting members. The nine provinces each have their own unicameral assemblies. For historical reasons political support in the country has been sequestered by the principal actors in that history, such as the African National Congress in much of the country and the Inkatha Freedom Party in KwaZulu-Natal, though more recently dissatisfaction with the pace of change away from the apartheid era's inequalities and disproportions of economic influence have produced political groupings different from these. As with the system in which its roots lie, South Africa does not have an institutional separation of the executive and legislative powers.

A contrast to these Westminster Model or model-derived polities is offered by France. France's bicameral legislature consists of a 577-member National Assembly and a 348-member Senate elected indirectly by about 150,000 *grands électeurs* who are municipal officials, mayors, and councillors, and members of the National Assembly. Members of the National Assembly, known as deputies, are elected by a two-round run-off system to represent a single-member constituency. No member of the Assembly can hold a ministerial post while sitting as a deputy; if a deputy accepts a ministerial post he or she must vacate the seat for a substitute, resuming the seat on quitting ministerial office. Ministers are required to attend the Assembly to answer questions and hear debate on legislation they are proposing.

The President is elected separately, for a five-year term, in a run-off system which notionally results in him (or her) having, by the end of the process, majority support in the country. The Prime Minister is appointed by the President, and in turn appoints a ministry. When President and Prime Minister are from the same party the President's role is an influential one; when the majority in the Assembly belongs to a different party the resulting 'cohabitation' can be tense. The President chairs the Council of Ministers and is head of the military. A presidential term is five years and the maximum number of possible terms is two. The executive and legislature are separate institutions; the judiciary is constitutionally protected from interference by the executive, and is a career profession for which its members are vocationally trained – that is, not drawn from the ranks of practising advocates.

Another contrast is offered by Germany. The electoral system for the Bundestag is a mixed-member proportional system designed to prevent a single party from having a majority over all other parties in Parliament, thus obliging the formation of coalitions, though in practice the two main parties, the Christian Democratic Union and the Social Democratic Party, have dominated, usually with support from the liberal centrist Free Democratic Party which for a considerable period after the Second World War held the balance. More recently other parties, such as the Greens, have come to prominence, disturbing the triopoly. Although the Chancellor and a number of federal ministers might be members of the Bundestag, they are not required to be so. The Chancellor is elected by the Bundestag, and proposes candidates for ministerial positions to the President – a constitutional formality. As a federal state the upper house of the bicameral legislature, the Bundesrat, represents the sixteen regional states (the *Lander*). Its members are delegates of their state governments (not Parliaments), representing the position taken by those governments regarding federal matters. Their numbers are *degressively* proportional to the populations of their states, that is, distributed in a way that favours smaller-population states. Members from a state must vote together as a single bloc, as required by their state governments. The Bundesrat plays an important role in the legislative process in Germany; legislation has to be agreed by it – that is, by the states – before being passed to the Bundestag.

APPENDIX IV:

BRITISH PARLIAMENTARY CODE OF CONDUCT

House of Commons Code of Conduct

Approved by the House of Commons on 12 March 2012, 17 March 2015 and 19 July 2018
Ordered by the House of Commons to be printed 24 July 2018
Published on 1 August 2018 by authority of the House of Commons HC 1474

Contents

Honesty
Leadership
Parliamentary Behaviour Code
V. Rules of Conduct
VI. Upholding the Code

The Code of Conduct for Members of Parliament

Prepared pursuant to the Resolution of the House of 19 July 1995

I. Purpose of the Code

1. The purpose of this Code of Conduct is to assist all Members in the discharge of their obligations to the House, their constituents and the public at large by:
a) establishing the standards and principles of conduct expected of all Members in undertaking their duties;
b) setting the rules of conduct which underpin these standards and principles and to which all Members must adhere; and in so doing
c) ensuring public confidence in the standards expected of all Members and in the commitment of the House to upholding these rules.

II. Scope of the Code

1. The Code applies to Members in all aspects of their public life. It does not seek to regulate what Members do in their purely private and personal lives.
2. The obligations set out in this Code are complementary to those which apply to all Members by virtue of the procedural and other rules of the House and the rulings of the Chair, and to

those which apply to Members falling within the scope of the Ministerial Code.

III. Duties of Members

4. By virtue of the oath, or affirmation, of allegiance taken by all Members when they are elected to the House, Members have a duty to be faithful and bear true allegiance to Her Majesty the Queen, her heirs and successors, according to law.
5. Members have a duty to uphold the law, including the general law against discrimination.
6. Members have a general duty to act in the interests of the nation as a whole; and a special duty to their constituents.
7. Members should act on all occasions in accordance with the public trust placed in them. They should always behave with probity and integrity, including in their use of public resources.

IV. General Principles of Conduct

8. In carrying out their parliamentary and public duties, Members will be expected to observe the following general principles of conduct identified by the Committee on Standards in Public Life in its First Report as applying to holders of public office.* These principles will be taken into account when considering the investigation and determination of any allegations of breaches of the rules of conduct in Part V of the Code.

"Selflessness
Holders of public office should take decisions solely in terms of the public interest. They should not do so in order to gain

---

* Cm 2850–I, p 14

financial or other material benefits for themselves, their family, or their friends.

Integrity
Holders of public office should not place themselves under any financial or other obligation to outside individuals or organizations that might influence them in the performance of their official duties.

Objectivity
In carrying out public business, including making public appointments, awarding contracts, or recommending individuals for rewards and benefits, holders of public office should make choices on merit.

Accountability
Holders of public office are accountable for their decisions and actions to the public and must submit themselves to whatever scrutiny is appropriate to their office.

Openness
Holders of public office should be as open as possible about all the decisions and actions that they take. They should give reasons for their decisions and restrict information only when the wider public interest clearly demands.

Honesty
Holders of public office have a duty to declare any private interests relating to their public duties and to take steps to resolve any conflicts arising in a way that protects the public interest.

Leadership

Holders of public office should promote and support these principles by leadership and example."

Parliamentary Behaviour Code

9. Members are also expected to observe the principles set out in the Parliamentary Behaviour Code of respect, professionalism, understanding others' perspectives, courtesy, and acceptance of responsibility.

V. Rules of Conduct

10. Members are expected to observe the following rules and associated Resolutions of the House.

11. Members shall base their conduct on a consideration of the public interest, avoid conflict between personal interest and the public interest and resolve any conflict between the two, at once, and in favour of the public interest.

12. No Member shall act as a paid advocate in any proceeding of the House.*

13. The acceptance by a Member of a bribe to influence his or her conduct as a Member, including any fee, compensation or reward in connection with the promotion of, or opposition to, any Bill, Motion, or other matter submitted, or intended to be submitted to the House, or to any Committee of the House, is contrary to the law of Parliament.†

---

* Resolutions of 6 November 1995 and 15 July 1947 as amended on 6 November 1995 and 14 May 2002
† Resolutions of 2 May 1695, 22 June 1858, and 15 July 1947 as amended on 6 November 1995 and 14 May 2002

14. Members shall fulfil conscientiously the requirements of the House in respect of the registration of interests in the Register of Members' Financial Interests. They shall always be open and frank in drawing attention to any relevant interest in any proceeding of the House or its Committees, and in any communications with Ministers, Members, public officials or public office holders.[*]

15. Information which Members receive in confidence in the course of their parliamentary duties should be used only in connection with those duties. Such information must never be used for the purpose of financial gain.

16. Members are personally responsible and accountable for ensuring that their use of any expenses, allowances, facilities and services provided from the public purse is in accordance with the rules laid down on these matters. Members shall ensure that their use of public resources is always in support of their parliamentary duties. It should not confer any undue personal or financial benefit on themselves or anyone else, or confer undue advantage on a political organization.

17. Members shall never undertake any action which would cause significant damage to the reputation and integrity of the House of Commons as a whole, or of its Members generally.

Respect
18. A Member must treat their staff and all those visiting or working for or with Parliament with dignity, courtesy and respect.

---

[*] Resolutions of the House of 22 May 1974 as amended on 9 February 2009; 12 June 1975 as amended on 19 July 1995 and 9 February 2009; 12 June 1975 as amended on 9 February 2009; 17 December 1985 as amended on 9 February 2009; 6 November 1995 as amended on 14 May 2002 and 9 February 2009; 13 July 1992; 30 April 2009 as amended on 7 February 2011; and 27 March 2008, as amended on 9 February 2009

VI. Upholding the Code

19. The application of this Code shall be a matter for the House of Commons, and particularly for the Committee on Standards and the Parliamentary Commissioner for Standards acting in accordance with Standing Orders Nos 149 and 150 respectively.

20. The Commissioner may investigate a specific matter relating to a Member's adherence to the rules of conduct under the Code. Members shall cooperate, at all stages, with any such investigation by or under the authority of the House. No Member shall lobby a member of the Committee in a manner calculated or intended to influence its consideration of an alleged breach of this Code.

21. The Committee will consider any report from the Commissioner to it and report its conclusions and recommendations to the House. The House may impose a sanction on the Member where it considers it necessary.

BIBLIOGRAPHY

All website references were accurate as at 13 August 2019.

'An Agreement of the People (1647)', https://en.wikisource.org/wiki/ An_Agreement_of_the_People_(1647)

An Authentic Copy of the New Plan of the French Constitution, as Presented to the National Convention, by the Committee of Constitution (London: J. Debrett, 1793)

Kenneth Arrow, 'A Difficulty in the Concept of Social Welfare', *Journal of Political Economy*, Volume 58, Issue 4 (1950), https://www.stat.uchicago. edu/~lekheng/meetings/mathofranking/ref/arrow.pdf

Isaac Asimov, 'The Cult of Ignorance', *Newsweek*, 21 January 1980

Clement Attlee, 'July Election Nearer', *The Times*, 22 May 1945

Jacques-Bénigne Bossuet, *Politics Drawn from the Very Words of Holy Scripture* (1709), ed. Patrick Riley (Cambridge: Cambridge University Press, 1990, 1999)

Vernon Bogdanor, *The New British Constitution* (London: Hart Publishing, 2009)

Henry Brooke, 'The History of Judicial Independence in England and Wales' (2015), https://sirhenrybrooke.me/2015/11/03/the-history-of-judicial- independence-in-england-and-wales/

Edmund Burke, 'Speech to the Electors of Bristol' (3 November 1774), in *The Works of the Right Honourable Edmund Burke* (London: Henry G. Bohn, 1854–6), vol. 1, pp. 446–8

Carole Cadwalladr, 'Revealed: How US Billionaire Helped to Back Brexit', *Observer*, 26 February 2017, https://www.theguardian.com/politics/ 2017/feb/26/us-billionaire-mercer-helped-back-brexit

A. J. Carlyle, *A History of Medieval Political Theory in the West* (Edinburgh and London: Blackwood & Sons, 1903)

Center for Deliberative Democracy, http://cdd.stanford.edu

Cicero, *De Legibus*, trans. C. W. Keyes, Loeb Classical Library (Cambridge, Mass: Harvard University Press, 1951)

Nicolas de Condorcet (Marquis de Condorcet), *Sketch of a Historical Picture of the Progress of the Human Spirit* (1795)

Benjamin Constant, *Political Writings*, ed. Biancamaria Fontana (Cambridge: Cambridge University Press, 1988)

Drew Desilver, 'House Seats Rarely Flip from One Party to the Other', Pew Research Center (2016), https://www.pewresearch.org/fact-tank/2016/09/07/house-seats-rarely-flip-from-one-party-to-the-other/

A. V. Dicey, *Introduction to the Study of the Law of the Constitution* (8th Edition with new Introduction) (London: Macmillan, 1915)

John Dunn, *Setting the People Free: The Story of Democracy* (London: Atlantic Books, 2006)

Ronald Dworkin, *Taking Rights Seriously* (Cambridge, Mass: Harvard University Press, 1977)

Electoral Reform Society, *Westminster Beyond Brexit: Ending the Politics of Division* (2019)

Adam Ferguson, *An Essay on the History of Civil Society* (Edinburgh: T. Cadell; and W. Creech, and J. Bell, 1782)

Thomas Ferguson, *Golden Rule: The Investment Theory of Party Competition* (Chicago/London: University of Chicago Press, 1995)

James Fishkin, *When the People Speak: Deliberative Democracy and Public Consultation* (Oxford: Oxford University Press, 2009)

Ronald Formisano, *Plutocracy in America* (Baltimore: Johns Hopkins University Press, 2019)

Foundation for Future Generations, 'German-speaking Community of Belgium Becomes World's First Region with Permanent Citizen Participation Drafted by Lot' (2019), https://www.foundationfuturegenerations.org/files/documents/news/20190226_dgpermanentcitizensassembly_pressrelease.pdf

Anatole France, *Le Lys Rouge* (Paris: Calmann-Lévy, 1894); *The Red Lily*, trans. Winifred Stephens (London: Bodley Head, 1908, 1930)

Robert Frank, 'Richest 1% Now Owns Half the World's Wealth', *CNBC*, 14 November 2017, https://www.cnbc.com/2017/11/14/richest-1-per-cent-now-own-half-the-worlds-wealth.html

Mark Funkhouser, 'The Real Purpose of Government', *Governing*, October 2015, https://www.governing.com/gov-institute/on-leadership/gov-government-purpose-capitalism.html

BIBLIOGRAPHY

J. K. Galbraith, *The New Industrial State* (London: Hamish Hamilton, 1967)
— *The Good Society* (New York: Houghton Mifflin, 1996)
Andrew Gamble and Tony Wright, *Rethinking Democracy* (London: Political Quarterly Publishing, 2019)
Martin Gilens and Benjamin I. Page, 'Testing Theories of American Politics: Elites, Interest Groups, and Average Citizens', *Perspectives on Politics*, Volume 12, Issue 3, September 2014, https://scholar.princeton.edu/sites/default/files/mgilens/files/gilens_and_page_2014_-testing_theories_of_american_politics.doc.pdf
W. E. Gladstone, *Gleanings of Past Years* (London: John Murray, 1879)
A. C. Grayling, *Democracy and Its Crisis* (London: Oneworld, 2017)
— *The History of Philosophy* (London: Viking, 2019)
Lord Hailsham, 'Elective Dictatorship', *The Listener*, 21 October 1976
Han Fei, *Han Feizi: Basic Writings*, trans. Burton Watson (New York: Columbia University Press, 2003)
Isabel Hardman, *Why We Get the Wrong Politicians* (London: Atlantic Books, 2018)
David Held, *Models of Democracy* (Cambridge: Polity Press, 2006)
Thomas Hobbes, *Leviathan* (1651), Clarendon Edition of the Works of Thomas Hobbes, Volume 1 (Oxford: Clarendon Press, 2012)
House of Commons Briefing Paper 07212, 3 June 2015, https://research-briefings.files.parliament.uk/documents/CBP-7212/CBP-7212.pdf
House of Commons Code of Conduct HC 1474, https://publications.parliament.uk/pa/cm201719/cmcode/1474/1474.pdf
Ivor Jennings, *The Law and the Constitution*, 5th ed. (London: University of London Press, 1961)
Joshua L. Kalla and David E. Broockman, 'Campaign Contributions Facilitate Access to Congressional Officials: A Randomized Field Experiment', *American Journal of Political Science*, Volume 60, Issue 3, July 2016
J. P. Kenyon, *The Stuart Constitution* (Cambridge: Cambridge University Press, 1996)
Charles Kesler (ed.), *The Federalist Papers* (New York: Signet Classics, 2003)
Ralph Ketcham (ed.), *The Anti-Federalist Papers* (New York: Signet Classics, 2003)
Anthony King and Ivor Crewe, *The Blunders of our Government* (London: Oneworld, 2014)
Philip B. Kurland, 'The Rise and Fall of the Doctrine of Separation of Powers', *Michigan Law Review*, Volume 85, Issue 592, December 1986
Ursula K. Le Guin, 'The Ones Who Walk Away from Omelas', in *New Dimensions 3*, ed. Robert Silverberg (New York: Doubleday, 1973)

Steven Levitsky and Daniel Ziblatt, *How Democracies Die* (New York: Penguin Random House, 2018)

Livy, *Ab Urbe Condita*, trans. B. O. Foster (Cambridge, Mass: Loeb Classical Library, Harvard, 1919)

John Locke, *Two Treatises of Government* (1689) (Cambridge: Cambridge University Press, 1988)

Jolyon Maugham, 'Now the Judges Agree – the Vote for Brexit Was Clearly Tainted', *Guardian*, 14 September 2018, https://www.theguardian.com/commentisfree/2018/sep/14/judges-brexit-vote-eu-referendum-vote-leave

Charles H. McIlwain, *The Growth of Political Thought in the West: From the Greeks to the End of the Middle Ages* (1932) (New York: Cooper Square Publishers, 1969)

— *Constitutionalism Ancient and Modern* (Ithaca: Cornell University Press, 1940)

Iain McLean, *What's Wrong with the British Constitution* (Oxford: Oxford University Press, 2010)

Charles Mill, *The Racial Contract* (Ithaca: Cornell University Press, 2014)

John Stuart Mill, *Considerations on Representative Government* (London: Parker, Son & Bourn, 1861)

James Miller, *Can Democracy Work?: A Short History of a Radical Idea, from Ancient Athens to Our World* (London: Oneworld, 2018)

John Miller, *The Glorious Revolution*, 8th impression (London: Longman, 1983)

Baron de Montesquieu, *The Spirit of the Laws* (1748), trans. Anne Cohler, Basia Miller, and Harold Stone (Cambridge: Cambridge University Press, 1989)

Michael Morreau, 'Arrow's Theorem', in *The Stanford Encyclopedia of Philosophy* (Winter 2016 Edition), ed. Edward N. Zalta, https://plato.stanford.edu/entries/arrows-theorem/

National Council of State Legislatures (NCSL) 'Separation of Powers – An Overview', 1 May 2019, http://www.ncsl.org/research/about-state-legislatures/separation-of-powers-an-overview.aspx

Robert Nozick, *Anarchy, State and Utopia* (New York: Basic Books, 1974)

James O'Brien, 'Brexit Referendum Was Corruptly Won, but Result Stands Thanks to Loophole', *LBC*, 25 February 2019, https://www.lbc.co.uk/radio/presenters/james-obrien/brexit-referendum-corruptly-won-but-result-stands/

Thomas Paine, *The Rights of Man* (1791) (New York: Penguin Books, 1985)

Parliament of Australia, 'Parliament and Government', https://www.aph.gov.au/About_Parliament/Work_of_the_Parliament/Forming_and_Governing_a_Nation/parl

Parliamentary Voting System and Constituencies Act 2011, http://www.legislation.gov.uk/ukpga/2011/1/contents/enacted

Carole Pateman, *The Sexual Contract* (Oxford: Polity Press, 1988)

Walter Pater, *Studies in the Renaissance* (1888) (Oxford: Oxford University Press, 2010)

William Rivers Pitt, 'Trump's War on the Constitution Has Reached a Breaking Point', *Truthout*, 22 May 2019, https://truthout.org/articles/trumps-war-on-the-constitution-has-reached-a-breaking-point

Polybius, *The Histories*, trans. Brian McGing (Oxford: Oxford University Press, 2010)

John Rawls, *A Theory of Justice* (Cambridge, Mass: Harvard University Press, 1971)

Suzanne Robbins, 'Money in Elections Doesn't Mean What You Think It Does', *The Conversation*, 29 October 2018, http://theconversation.com/money-in-elections-doesnt-mean-what-you-think-it-does-104452

Henry St John, 1st Viscount Bolingbroke, 'Dissertation on Parties', in *The Craftsman* (1735), https://archive.org/details/adissertationup00amhugoog/page/n6

Ian Shapiro, *The State of Democratic Theory* (Princeton: Princeton University Press, 2003)

Peter Singer, 'Why Vote?', Project Syndicate, December 2007, https://www.utilitarian.net/singer/by/200712--.htm

M. Skjonsberg, 'Lord Bolingbroke's Theory of Party and Opposition', *Historical Journal*, Volume 59, Issue 4, December 2016

Sir Leslie Stephen, *The Science of Ethics* (London: Smith, Elder, 1882)

Iain Stewart, 'Men of Class: Aristotle, Montesquieu and Dicey on "Separation of Powers" and the "Rule of Law"', *Macquarie Law Journal*, Volume 4, January 2004

David A. Strauss, 'What is Constitutional Theory?', *California Law Review*, Volume 87, Issue 581, May 1999

Gemma Tetlow and Alex Stojanovic, 'Understanding the Economic Impact of Brexit', November 2018, https://www.instituteforgovernment.org.uk/sites/default/files/Economic%20impact%20of%20Brexit%20summary.pdf

E. R. Turner, 'The Development of the Cabinet 1688–1760', *American Historical Review*, Volume 18, Issue 4, July 1913

François Marie Arouet de Voltaire, *Letters on the English* (1733), https://www.bartleby.com/34/2/

Jeremy Waldron (ed.), *Nonsense Upon Stilts: Bentham, Burke and Marx on the Rights of Man* (New York: Methuen, 1987)

David Williams, *Condorcet and Modernity* (Cambridge: Cambridge University Press, 2004)

C. Witko, 'Campaign Contributions, Access, and Government Contracting', *Journal of Public Administration Research and Theory*, Volume 21, Issue 4, October 2011

Christian Wolmar, *The Great Railway Revolution* (London: Atlantic Books, 2012)

Xunzi, *Basic Writings*, trans. Burton Watson (New York: Columbia University Press, 2003)

NOTES

Preface

1 A. C. Grayling, *Democracy and Its Crisis* (2017).
2 I comment on these alternative forms of democracy in Appendix II.
3 In chapter 5 I touch on the debate about the uncodified constitutional arrangements, such as they are, in the United Kingdom, and the difficulties posed by the United States Constitution's inflexibility, by way of illustration of practical problems which reveal the deficits of principle that cause them.
4 See Appendix II.

Introduction

1 The considerations speak not only to other Westminster or Westminster-derived models, but to non-Westminster forms of democracy also; the comparisons and similarities among all democratic systems are telling.
2 See Appendix II.
3 Livy, *Ab Urbe Condita* (1919), p. 219.
4 Jacques-Bénigne Bossuet, *Politics Drawn from the Very Words of Holy Scripture* (1709). 'But kings, although their power comes from on high, as has been said, should not regard themselves as masters of that power to use it at their pleasure . . . they must employ it with fear and self-restraint, as a thing coming from God and of which God will demand an account.'
5 John Stuart Mill, *Considerations on Representative Government* (1861), chapter 5.

6 Voltaire, *Letters on the English* (1733); see Letters VIII and IX.

7 Han Fei, *Han Feizi* (2003). To quote Han Fei's story of the hare is not to approve everything in his views, as will appear later.

8 'Perfectibilism' (the possibility of achieving perfection) was part of the great Enlightenment debate in which it was contrasted with 'meliorism' (the more modest possibility of improving things).

9 Libertarianism is about maximizing licence for individual and corporate activity to pursue self-identified interests. Liberalism is about valorizing civil liberties while correlatively respecting moral demands for a humane and inclusive society. To put the point tendentiously: the distinction lies in competing construals of 'liberty'. In one view it means licence, including in practical terms the licence to ignore the rights of others in advancing one's own interests; in the other it means a right that others possess too and must be respected in all.

1 What *Democracy* Entails

1 I Identify the dilemma of democracy and the right to 'good enough' government in *Democracy and Its Crisis*.

2 One can grant that not all non-democracies are tyrannical, and that civil liberties and human rights can be respected in political arrangements other than democracies. Arguably, however, the benefits are intrinsic to democracy but adventitious in other systems, where they would depend upon, for example, the goodwill of the current ruler or the strength of a dominant tradition such as a religion.

3 The example of electoral reform in the UK is a good illustration of this. The architects of the US Constitution were careful to place a series of filters between the popular will and the offices of legislation and government, largely to achieve a solution to the 'Plato problem' about the fitness of the enfranchised to dispose of power.

4 Efforts to reduce the property qualification in Virginia were resisted by those who held it until seventy years later, in 1851. The state was accordingly run by wealthy landowners in its relatively unpopulated eastern regions while its more populous and poorer western regions went largely unrepresented.

5 John Locke, *Two Treatises of Government* (1689). In the *Second Treatise* §§119–22 Locke considers 'what shall be understood to be *a sufficient declaration of a Man's consent, to make him subject* to the Laws of any Government' [italics as in text]. The discussion might seem puzzling

because it concludes that nothing can make people 'Subjects or Members of [a] Commonwealth' other than their 'actually entering into it by positive Engagement, and express Promise and Compact'. His 'submitting to the Laws of any Country, living quietly, enjoying Privileges and Protection under them, *makes not a Man a Member of that Society*: this is only a local Protection and Homage' of the kind enjoyed by a foreigner living in a country without being a citizen of it. On the face of it the first assertion would seem to require an explicit and positive act of giving consent to being ruled by a government – by voting, say; but Locke does not espouse democracy, and therefore does not go so far as to consider what would be the status of anyone not enfranchised – namely, women, who would not be 'Subjects or Members' because in any then connoted circumstances they would be excluded from giving active consent. Locke's point, however, is not that *consent to being* governed requires a 'positive engagement'; *that* consent is implicitly contained in 'submitting to the government' while enjoying its protection (§121). Once the protection is over – either by the individual moving to another country, or the government's failure to provide it – the individual no longer 'submits to the government'. The 'positive engagement' applies to a different matter: not to consenting to be governed, but to *being a member of the commonwealth*. And this 'positive engagement' is not achieved by (say) voting or some cognate act, but by *the original contract* which concerns 'the beginning of Political Societies' (§122). Quite how this constitutes an 'express Promise and Compact' entered into by any individual subsequent to the making of the original contract is not explained.

6 Mill, *Representative Government*, chapter 8.

7 Isaac Asimov, 'The Cult of Ignorance' (1980), p. 19.

8 This is the overwhelming fault of referendums also, which in any case are not native to representative democracy and should only be used, if ever, in cases where a very basic – in reality, crude – either-or choice is possible.

9 In a different way, though, minoritarian super-influence is a continuous danger also in Westminster Model democracies operating FPTP electoral systems that produce two-party dominance; see chapter 5.

10 The full text of the 'Putney Debates' may be read at 'An Agreement of the People (1647)', https://en.wikisource.org/wiki/An_Agreement_of_the_People_(1647).

11 See Grayling, *Democracy and Its Crisis*, chapters 4 and 5 *passim* for an account of this development. Aristotle's approach to solving Plato's problems focused on what I here call the 'informal' side of the question, that

is, on the people and practices of the political order. The theories developed in the modern period focused on the formal – institutional – side.

12 Ibid., chapters 6 and 7.

13 Edmund Burke, 'Speech to the Electors of Bristol' (1774).

14 The UK and the European Court of Human Rights wrangled over the question of prisoners' suffrage for many years before a partial resolution was found.

15 This point was made by former New Zealand Prime Minister Sir Geoffrey Palmer in discussion with the author.

16 Ian Shapiro, *The State of Democratic Theory* (2003), p. 1.

17 John Dunn, *Setting the People Free: The Story of Democracy* (2006).

18 Shapiro, *The State of Democratic Theory*, p. 5.

2 The Purpose of Government

1 An exception to most current models is China, where unbridled economic liberties are allowed to some, but no political liberties to any, and where inequality is allowed to grow unchecked, as something to be praised at least in those who have the Party's approval. The hybrid that is China's economy and society reprises absolutisms of the past. The Party is like a charioteer using vicious curb-bits when necessary but allowing the horses to run wild as long as they serve his purpose.

2 Summary accounts of the views of Hobbes, Locke, and Rousseau are given in Grayling, *Democracy and Its Crisis*, chapters 4 and 5, and of Rawls in Grayling, *The History of Philosophy* (2019), pp. 458–62.

3 John Rawls, *A Theory of Justice* (1971), pp. 97, 212–13.

4 Thomas Hobbes, *Leviathan* (1651), Book II, chapters 17–19.

5 Locke, *Second Treatise*, §143.

6 Robert Nozick, *Anarchy, State and Utopia* (1974). A summary of the view is provided in Grayling, *The History of Philosophy*, pp. 462–6.

7 Mill, *Considerations on Representative Government*, p. 176.

8 See Carole Pateman, *The Sexual Contract* (1988), and Charles Mill, *The Racial Contract* (2014); their views are analogous.

9 Ronald Dworkin, *Taking Rights Seriously* (1977), p. 370.

10 Mark Funkhouser, 'The Real Purpose of Government' (2015).

11 In practice, the operation of capitalism in democracies, with the latter's emphasis on individual liberty and protection of private property, results in gross disproportions in the distribution of wealth. For example, in the UK more than 50% of land is owned by 1% of the population. In the

world at large 50% of global wealth is own by 1% of the world's population. Robert Frank, 'Richest 1% Now Owns Half the World's Wealth' (2017).

12 Even for *one* to suffer: see Ursula K. Le Guin, 'The Ones Who Walk Away from Omelas' (1973), a short story first published in *New Dimensions 3*, ed. Robert Silverberg. In the blissful utopia of Omelas the great good and happiness of the citizens depends on the continuing suffering of a single child in a dungeon. All citizens, on coming of age, are apprised of this fact. Despite the initial horror most of them feel, they soon come to accept the utilitarian advantage to the entire populace of one child's torments. Some, however, walk away from Omelas: the final sentence says, 'The place they go towards is a place even less imaginable to most of us than the city of happiness. I cannot describe it at all. It is possible it does not exist. But they seem to know where they are going, the ones who walk away from Omelas.' Indeed.

13 See 'Political Thought in the Renaissance', in Grayling, *The History of Philosophy*, pp. 185–92.

14 See J. K. Galbraith, *The New Industrial State* (1967) and *The Good Society* (1996).

3 Powers and Institutions

1 Baron de Montesquieu, *Spirit of the Laws* (1748), Book XI, chapter VI.

2 Ibid.

3 Locke, *Second Treatise*, §§159, 143.

4 Ibid., §§145–6.

5 J. P. Kenyon, *The Stuart Constitution* (1996), p. 445, and John Miller, *The Glorious Revolution* (1983), pp. 101–2. Quoted in Henry Brooke, 'The History of Judicial Independence in England and Wales' (2015).

6 Iain Stewart, 'Men of Class: Aristotle, Montesquieu and Dicey on "Separation of Powers" and the "Rule of Law"' (2004), p. 198.

7 Charles Kesler (ed.), *Federalist Papers* (2003), no. 47, p. 298.

8 National Council of State Legislatures (NCSL), 'Separation of Powers – An Overview' (2019).

9 Ivor Jennings, *The Law and the Constitution* (1961), p. 61.

10 An example is the situation that obtained in the UK in 2018–19.

11 Locke unequivocally condemns any such practice. 'The people kept *for themselves* the choice of their representatives, as the fences around their properties; and the only reason they could have for this was so that the

representatives would always be freely chosen, and – having been chosen – would freely act and advise in ways that they judged, after examination and mature debate, to be necessary for the commonwealth and the public good. Representatives can't do this if they have given their votes in advance, before hearing the debate and weighing the reasons on all sides. For someone to prepare such a legislative assembly as *this*, and try to set up the declared supporters of his own will as the true representatives of the people and the law-makers of the society, is certainly as great a breach of trust, and as complete an admission that he plans to subvert the government, as could be met with.' Locke, *Second Treatise*, chapter 19, §222.

12 E. R. Turner, 'The Development of the Cabinet 1688–1760' (1913).

13 The last member of the House of Lords to serve as Prime Minister while in the Lords was the 3rd Marquis of Salisbury, serving in the role three times: 1885–6, 1886–92, and 1895–1902. When the 14th Earl of Home became Prime Minister in 1963 he renounced his peerage and stood for the House of Commons, serving as Prime Minister under the name Sir Alec Douglas-Home. He afterwards returned to the House of Lords as a life peer with the title Baron Home of the Hirsel. 'Home' is pronounced 'Hume'.

14 W. E. Gladstone, *Gleanings of Past Years* (1879), vol. 1, p. 244.

15 Whenever a body such as the Electoral Commission or the Press Complaints Commission in the UK is criticized for not having 'teeth', what is meant is that the powers it possesses do not match its function, thus rendering it ineffective or relatively so. As a rule it would be appropriate for such bodies to have the degree of power necessary to make fulfilment of their functions possible. The fact that this is not so marks a characteristic of governments: wishing to be seen to be doing something or addressing a concern, but reluctant to go the whole way of delegating the commensurate authority. Here the power–function distinction is painfully marked.

16 'it is only the roughness of the eye that makes any two things seem alike', said Walter Pater, *Studies in the Renaissance* (1888), Conclusion.

17 This point is discussed in detail in Grayling, *Democracy and Its Crisis*, Part II.

18 Defence of this aspect of the Westminster Model was eloquently made by Lord Lisvane, former Clerk to the House of Commons, in conversation with the author. The home page of the Australian Parliament cites it as a virtue of the system that the executive is drawn from the legislative majority for this reason; it states, 'The most distinctive feature of the

House is that the party or group with majority support in the House forms the Government. The accountability of the Government is illustrated every sitting day, especially during Question Time'. Parliament of Australia, 'Parliament and Government'.

19 Lord Hailsham, 'Elective Dictatorship' (1976).
20 Sir Leslie Stephen, *The Science of Ethics* (1882), p. 145. The constitutional commentator A. V. Dicey quoted this – he was, incidentally, Stephen's cousin – with approval in his discussion of parliamentary sovereignty. A. V. Dicey, *Introduction to the Study of the Law of the Constitution* (1915).

4 Politics and People

1 This, arguably, is exactly what has happened in the UK, as the Brexit referendum testifies.
2 Steven Levitsky and Daniel Ziblatt, *How Democracies Die* (2018), p. 8.
3 Mill, *Representative Government*, pp. 139–40.
4 Levitsky and Ziblatt, *How Democracies Die*, pp. 35–8.
5 There has been only one occasion on which a sufficient number of 'faithless Electors' refused to support a candidate; he was Richard M. Johnson, who had won nomination as Vice President in 1836.
6 Levitsky and Ziblatt, *How Democracies Die*, p. 40.
7 Kesler (ed.), *Federalist Papers* no. 10, pp. 71–9.
8 Ibid.
9 Ibid.
10 Ibid.
11 See Grayling, *Democracy and Its Crisis*, chapter 9 *passim*.
12 Kesler (ed.), *Federalist Papers* no. 51, p. 316.
13 A scene in Monty Python's *Life of Brian* satirizing the propensities of political movements (and likewise religions and all other interest groups) to repeated fission, with greater hostility obtaining between the separated parts than they bear to official opponents, sums this up to perfection.
14 House of Commons Code of Conduct HC 1474, printed in full as Appendix IV.
15 They do it with relative impunity only in exceptional circumstances, as in the period of chaos during the minority Conservative administration of Theresa May in 2018–19.
16 Gemma Tetlow and Alex Stojanovic, 'Understanding the Economic Impact of Brexit' (2018), is just one of a number of studies of this. Any of the votes supporting the Conservative Party policy of Brexit can be

adduced as support by MPs for harming the national economy and the citizens who would lose jobs, homes, opportunities, or public services as a result.

17 An example, despite the apparent implication of the title, is offered by Isabel Hardman's *Why We Get the Wrong Politicians* (2018). Her diagnosis of the problem with the institution is correct; she acknowledges the existence of 'yes-men' and inadequate scrutiny of legislation; and a number of her suggestions for improvements are good.

18 In the Trump case the universally negative character of these factors played little part in the outcome.

19 He called them 'bastards'.

20 James O'Brien, 'Brexit Referendum Was Corruptly Won, but Result Stands Thanks to Loophole' (2019).

21 This complex matter is treated in chapter 6.

22 *Hansard*, 16 June 2015.

23 It is not irrelevant to mention, in passing, that the editor of the flagship agenda-setting national daily news broadcast, Radio 4's *Today* programme, Sarah Sands, had held senior editorial appointments at two of the leading right-wing and pro-Brexit newspapers, the *Daily Mail* and the *Telegraph*, before joining Radio 4.

24 In Aristotle's definition of humanity, everyone is a *zoon politikon*; here I reserve the term for activists and politicians themselves.

5 Governance and Constitutionality

1 Kesler (ed.), *Federalist Papers*, no. 10. One of the influences on the founders of the new United States, a remarkable group of individuals whose reading, debates, and writings constitute a seminal moment in the development of political philosophy and practice, was the English statesman Henry St John, 1st Viscount Bolingbroke. He had been an influence on Montesquieu too, who had read him in the *Craftsman* journal and knew his other works. In his *Dissertation on Parties* Bolingbroke inveighed against factionalism and advocated national unity; the slogan 'not men, but measures' is associated with his name. It is a matter of controversy among scholars of eighteenth-century thought whether he was opposed to a system of parties as such; see M. Skjonsberg, 'Lord Bolingbroke's Theory of Party and Opposition' (2016), *passim*.

2 David Williams, *Condorcet and Modernity* (2004), p. 195. Condorcet's idea of local and regional assemblies from which delegates to a national

assembly would be drawn was intended to make democracy apply to the whole country and not just Paris. He opposed slavery, opposed the death penalty, championed individual liberty and the idea of progress, and was in favour of women's suffrage. He was an Enlightenment thinker who made significant contributions to mathematics, philosophy, and social theory. See also Condorcet's own *Sketch of a Historical Picture of the Progress of the Human Spirit* (1795).

3 *An Authentic Copy of the New Plan of the French Constitution, as Presented to the National Convention, by the Committee of Constitution* (1793), p. xlviii.

4 Respectively *United States v. Miller* 307 US 174 (1939) and *District of Columbia v. Heller* 07-290 (2008).

5 Following the excellent advice of New Zealand Prime Minister Jacinda Ardern in response to the massacre at the two mosques in Christchurch in March 2019, perpetrators of these atrocities should not be named, denying them the publicity they seek.

6 'Unbridled' might not always be the correct term. On the first day of the Battle of the Somme in 1916 the British suffered so many casualties – 40,000 on that day alone – that by the late afternoon many German troops ceased firing, no longer able to carry on shooting the slow-moving line-abreast soldiers staggering over open ground, easy and defenceless targets to be – quite literally – mown down.

7 Clement Attlee, 'July Election Nearer' (1945).

8 Parliamentary Voting System and Constituencies Act 2011, §8.

9 It is a matter of grave concern that these assessments were made some considerable time after the government decided to trigger a process for leaving the EU – that is, without a clear sense of the likely consequences. This is a failure of responsibility of an unconscionable kind.

10 *Hansard*, 16 June 2016.

11 Jolyon Maugham, 'Now the Judges Agree – the Vote for Brexit Was Clearly Tainted' (2018).

12 O'Brien, 'Brexit Referendum Was Corruptly Won'.

13 Thomas Paine, *The Rights of Man* (1791), chapter 1.

14 Ibid., chapter 7.

15 Ibid., chapter 13.

16 Writing just before the 200th anniversary of the US Constitution, Philip Kurland wrote, 'it is no slander to recognize that the 1787 document was born of prudent compromise rather than principle, that it derived more from experience than from doctrine, and that it was received with an ambivalence in no small part attributable to its ambiguities. Indeed, its

most stalwart supporters doubted its capacity for a long life. It should not be surprising, then, that even today there is disagreement over whether the Constitution of 1787 is now merely an artefact of late eighteenth-century American history or a *vade mecum* which has, in fact, controlled the allocation of government powers and the restraints on those powers throughout the two centuries since its birth.' Philip B. Kurland, 'The Rise and Fall of the Doctrine of Separation of Powers' (1986), p. 592.

6 Rights in a Democracy

1 The origins of the theory of natural rights is, however, considerably older: its source is the idea of natural human equality found in the Stoics and in Cicero and Seneca, a development sharply different from the Aristotelian view of natural human inequalities: see A. J. Carlyle, *A History of Medieval Political Theory in the West* (1903), pp. 8–9, and Charles H. McIlwain who observed that 'the idea of the equality of men is the profoundest contribution of the Stoics to political thought' in *The Growth of Political Thought in the West: From the Greeks to the End of the Middle Ages* (1932), pp. 114–15. In *De Legibus*, Book 1, section 28, Cicero says 'we are born for Justice, and that right is based, not upon opinions, but upon Nature'.

2 Jeremy Bentham, 'Anarchical Fallacies; being an examination of the Declaration of Rights issues during the French Revolution', in Jeremy Waldron (ed.), *Nonsense Upon Stilts: Bentham, Burke and Marx on the Rights of Man* (1987), p. 69.

3 Paine, *The Rights of Man*.

4 Accordingly, these considerations apply *mutatis mutandis* to animals in general.

5 Another point of difference with philosophical piety in this arena is that the imperative at work behind this point is a *hypothetical* one – 'if a person wishes to live her own life and have a chance to flourish *then* she must possess these rights.' Most philosophers are not satisfied with hypothetical imperatives; only categorical ones will do. But I suppose it must be left open to some eccentric individuals (perhaps like Pauline Réage's 'O') to dispense with liberty, privacy, human treatment, and the rest.

6 Christian Wolmar, *The Great Railway Revolution* (2012). See especially the discussion of corruption in the building of the transcontinental railway.

7 Adam Ferguson, *An Essay on the History of Civil Society* (1782), Part III, section II. The full quote reads: 'Every step and every movement of the multitude, even in what are termed enlightened ages, are made with equal blindness to the future; and nations stumble upon establishments, which are indeed the result of human action, but not the execution of any human design.'

8 Anatole France, *The Red Lily* (1930), pp. 117–18.

7 The Subversion of Democracy

1 Certain proportional systems, more for local and historical reasons than the voting method itself, can produce persisting two-party arrangements (and thus alternating one-party government); Australia is a case in point.

2 Johnny Mercer MP, @JohnnyMercerUK, 10.35 a.m., 11 April 2019.

3 That is, <17% is the proportion of the total electorate voting for explicitly Brexit-supporting parties, the Brexit Party and UKIP, *plus* the Conservative Party (but since some Conservatives were pro-EU the figure of 17% is an over-estimate).

4 In the 1970s UK governments of both left and right struggled to respond to the oil price hike that destabilized the world economy, and were unable to control industrial relations, the disputes in which – marking a fundamental rift in society about its direction and priorities – had a crippling effect on the national economy. Three-day working weeks, piles of uncollected rubbish in the streets, unburied bodies, ministers hastening to the IMF and World Bank cap in hand for bail-outs are searing memories of those days, from which membership of the EEC/EU did much to rescue the UK over the succeeding decades.

5 The UK government 2010–15 was a coalition between the Conservative Party and the Liberal Democratic Party, the latter very much in the minority and in a junior role. Its influence on major policy planks of the Conservative Party was restricted.

6 Ronald Formisano, *Plutocracy in America* (2019), p. 4.

7 Galbraith, *The Good Society*, p. 8.

8 Respectively 558 U.S. 310 (2010) and 581F.3d 1 (D.C. Cir. 2010).

9 Suzanne Robbins, 'Money in Elections Doesn't Mean What You Think It Does' (2018).

10 Martin Gilens and Benjamin I. Page, 'Testing Theories of American Politics: Elites, Interest Groups, and Average Citizens' (2014).

11 Ibid.

12 Joshua L. Kalla and David E. Broockman, 'Campaign Contributions Facilitate Access to Congressional Officials: A Randomized Field Experiment' (2016).

13 C. Witko, 'Campaign Contributions, Access, and Government Contracting' (2011).

14 Thomas Ferguson, *Golden Rule: The Investment Theory of Party Competition* (1995). Ferguson is the Director of Research at the Institute for New Economic Thinking (INET) in New York (https://www.ineteconomics.org).

15 It took action in court by the Good Law Project to get the Electoral Commission to investigate illegalities on the part of the Leave campaign in the 2016 EU referendum. The result was criminal charges against the Leave campaign, which was found guilty.

16 I reprise points here I make in *Democracy and Its Crisis*.

17 Aaron Banks on Twitter, 30 Jan. 2017, 3:38 pm: 'since we deployed this technology in leave.eu we got unprecedented levels of engagement. 1 video 13m views. AI won it for leave.' Arron Banks @Arron_banks.

18 Carole Cadwalladr, 'Revealed: How US Billionaire Helped to Back Brexit' (2017).

19 Ibid.

20 Ibid.

Conclusion

1 Examples at time of writing, however tendentious, in the British context might be given from all sides of politics: in my view the relentless and relentlessly trivializing aspect of the 24/7 news round had much to do with harassing and undermining the premiership of the thoughtful Gordon Brown, potentially a far better Prime Minister than he was allowed to be; Dominic Grieve had the most distinguished character and principles of anyone in the Conservative Party during the Brexit crisis, but far from having a chance to give the leadership he would assuredly have shown, he was instead threatened with deselection by his constituency party. A score of other examples might be cited, though it is a worrying reflection that out of 650 MPs so few stand out. The system keeps talent down and hidden.

Appendix I: Proportional Representation

1 For an account and discussion of Arrow's theorem, see Michael Morreau, 'Arrow's Theorem' (2016).
2 William Rivers Pitt, 'Trump's War on the Constitution Has Reached a Breaking Point' (2019).
3 In 2017 action was required in the UK Supreme Court to oblige the government to consult Parliament on triggering Article 50 of the Lisbon Treaty which initiated the Brexit process; in 2019 Boris Johnson's decision to prorogue Parliament to prevent MPs from stopping a 'no-deal' exit from the EU met with court actions, concerted efforts by opposition and governing party politicians, and widespread street protests across the country.

Appendix II: Alternative Forms of Democracy

1 A fuller summary of this can be found in Grayling, *The History of Philosophy*, pp. 534–53.
2 Xunzi, *Basic Writings*, trans. Burton Watson (2003), cf. p. 168.
3 Shapiro, *The State of Democratic Theory*.
4 Or the 'Rösti trench': German Swiss like a certain hash potato dish called *Rösti*, the French Swiss do not much favour it.
5 An even more striking example is Luxembourg, with a population of half a million and GDP per capita of $104,000 per annum.
6 London, with a population just slightly larger than Switzerland and a GDP per capita of $73,300, could by itself fit this model of an optimal state.
7 Polybius, *The Histories*, Book VI (2010).
8 Online petitions were introduced in the UK in November 2006 by the Labour Prime Minister Tony Blair.
9 This was the 2019 'Revoke Article 50' petition.
10 James Fishkin, *When the People Speak: Deliberative Democracy and Public Consultation* (2009).
11 See the Center for Deliberative Democracy website at http://cdd.stanford.edu.
12 Electoral Reform Society, *Westminster Beyond Brexit: Ending the Politics of Division* (2019).
13 See Foundation for Future Generations, 'German-speaking Community of Belgium Becomes World's First Region with Permanent Citizen Participation Drafted by Lot' (2019).

Appendix III: Some Westminster Model Systems

1 Strictly speaking Queen Elizabeth is the first of that name as queen of the UK; she is 'Elizabeth II' of England, Wales, and Northern Ireland, technically 'Elizabeth I' of everywhere else. But as the decorative part of the constitutions of her realms, the ordinal attached to her name maintains a link with the past and offers a focus for some degree of shared identity, two points that defenders of monarchy regard as cardinal.

2 This has of course always been controversial. One kind of argument urged against it is that one cannot claim of votes given under compulsion that they represent the consent of the people; this is a point made by Peter Singer, 'Why Vote?' (2007).

3 Drew Desilver, 'House Seats Rarely Flip from One Party to the Other' (2016).

INDEX

References to notes are indicated by n.

231